ELEMENTARY

John Hughes

Life Elementary Workbook

John Hughes

Publisher: Jason Mann

Publishing Consultant: Karen Spiller

Editorial Project Manager: Karen Spiller

Development Editor: Shona Rodger

Editor: Katy Wright

Contributing Writer: Nick Kenny (IELTS practice test)

Head of Marketing Communications: Ruth McAleavey

Strategic Marketing Manager: Michelle Cresswell

Project Editor: Amy Borthwick

Production Controller: Elaine Willis

National Geographic Liaison: Anna Kistin

Art Director: Natasa Arsenidou

Cover Design: Vasiliki Christoforidou

Text Design: Vasiliki Christoforidou

Compositor: Wild Apple Design Ltd

Audio: Prolingua Productions

© 2014 National Geographic Learning, a part of Cengage Learning

ALL RIGHTS RESERVED. No part of this work covered by the copyright herein may be reproduced, transmitted, stored or used in any form or by any means graphic, electronic, or mechanical, including but not limited to photocopying, recording, scanning, digitising, taping, Web distribution, information networks, or information storage and retrieval systems, except as permitted under Section 107 or 108 of the 1976 United States Copyright Act, or applicable copyright law of another jurisdiction, without the prior written permission of the publisher.

> For permission to use material from this text or product, submit all requests online at **cengage.com/permissions**
>
> Further permissions questions can be emailed to **permissionrequest@cengage.com**

ISBN: 978-1-133-31603-9

National Geographic Learning
Cheriton House, North Way, Andover, Hampshire SP10 5BE
United Kingdom

Cengage Learning is a leading provider of customised learning solutions with office locations around the globe, including Singapore, the United Kingdom, Australia, Mexico, Brazil and Japan. Locate our local office at **international.cengage.com/region**

Cengage Learning products are represented in Canada by Nelson Education Ltd.

Visit National Geographic Learning at **ngl.cengage.com**
Visit our corporate website at **www.cengage.com**

CREDITS

Although every effort has been made to contact copyright holders before publication, this has not always been possible. If notified, the publisher will undertake to rectify any errors or omissions at the earliest opportunity.

Text:
The publisher would like to thank the following sources for permission to reproduce their copyright protected text:

Tierney Thys for interview details. Reproduced with kind permission; National Geographic for extracts adapted from an interview with Josh Thome, Film-maker/Photographer; "Maui: Ten Places to Love", http://traveler.nationalgeographic.com; "Tshewang Wangchuk, Conservationist" by Waitt Grantee, www.nationalgeographic.com; Knicole Colón Astronomer", www.nationalgeographic.com; "Freshwater Hero: Shannon Switzer" http://environment.nationalgeographic.com; "Michael Lombardi Author/Environmentalist", www.nationalgeographic.com; and "Top 10 Food Road Trips", National Geographic Traveler, October 2010 and Drives of a Lifetime, copyright © National Geographic. Reproduced with permission; and Telegraph Media Group Limited for an extract from "Landmark cuckoo project reveals bird's migration mystery" by Roya Nikkhah in The Sunday Telegraph 6 May 2012, p.7, copyright © Telegraph Media Group Limited, 2012.

Photos:
The publishers would like to thank the following sources for permission to reproduce their copyright protected photographs:

Cover: (Simon Wong/Getty Images)

Inside: pp 4 (Brett Hobson), 5 (4Real/National Geographic Image Collection), 6 tl (Shutterstock), tm (Martin Shields/Alamy), 7 t (Shutterstock), bl (Shutterstock), 8 ml (Justin Guariglia/National Geographic Image Collection), bm (Shutterstock), 9 l (OJO Images Ltd/Alamy), r (Shutterstock), 10 tr (OJO Images Ltd/Alamy), ml (Shutterstock), ll (Shutterstock), 10 bl (Shutterstock), 12 (Pete Mcbride/National Geographic Image Collection), 13 (George F. Mobley/National Geographic Image Collection), 14 tl (AFP/Getty Images), tr (Jumbo Hostel), 16 b (incamerastock/Alamy), c (Alex Segre/Alamy), 16 d (Rolf Adlercreutz/Alamy), 18 turtle (Shutterstock), cheetah (Michael Nichols/National Geographic Image Collection), diamond ring (Shutterstock), plastic rings (PhotoAlto/Alamy), smart car (Graham Oliver/Alamy), stretch limo (Shutterstock), pen knife (Shutterstock), broken cup (Shutterstock), iPhone (FocusDigital/Alamy), rotary phone (Shutterstock), clock (Shutterstock), rollerblades (Shutterstock), bookshelf (Shutterstock), 20 (Sungjin Kim/National Geographic Image Collection), 23 tl (Shutterstock), tr (David Doubilet/National Geographic Image Collection), 26 (Debra Behr/Alamy), 27 (Andres Rodriguez/Alamy), 28 playing piano (Randy Olson/National Geographic Image Collection), people at cinema (Juice Images/Alamy), group of young people (Shutterstock), playing computer games (David J. Green – Lifestyle/Alamy), tae kwon do (Mason Trullinger/Alamy), playing tennis (Shutterstock), people hiking (Shutterstock), boy at gym (i love images/active/Alamy), r (Shutterstock), 30 ml (Tshewang Wangchuk), mr (Read Miller), bl (Knicole Colón), br (Michael Lombardi), 32 (Robert Harding World Imagery/Alamy), 34 (Visions of America/Universal Images Group/Getty Images), 37 cheese (Foodcollection.com/Alamy), pumpkin (Shutterstock), peaches (Shutterstock), shrimps (Shutterstock), crabs (Shutterstock), 38 (Wavebreak Media ltd/Alamy), 39 (Jochen Tack/Alamy), 40 (Space Frontiers/Archive Photos/Getty Images), 42 (Shutterstock), 43 chips (Shutterstock), mobile phone (Alex Segre/Alamy), restaurant bill (pixel shepherd/Alamy), lift (Shutterstock), pavement (Shutterstock), biscuit (Shutterstock), motorway (DBURKE/Alamy), petrol pump (Shutterstock), football (Colin Underhill/Alamy), full st (Shutterstock), 44 (Shutterstock), 45 (Ben Capp), 47 l (Juice Images/Alamy), r (Jon Foster), 48 (Benedicte Desrus/Alamy), 51 (Shutterstock), 52 tr (ClassicStock/Alamy), mr (Alberto Lowe/Reuters/Corbis), 53 (ITAR-TASS Photo Agency/Alamy), 54 tr (Frans Lanting/National Geographic Image Collection), mr (Shutterstock), br (James Forte/National Geographic Image Collection), 56 (Brian J. Skerry/National Geographic Image Collection), 57 (JurgaR/E+/Getty Images), 60 (Kenneth Garrett/National Geographic Image Collection), 61 l (20th Century Fox/The Kobal Collection), r (Carmen Morosan /National Geographic Image Collection), 62 a (Martin Gray/National Geographic Image Collection), b (Steve Raymer/National Geographic Image Collection), c (Bildagentur-online/McPhoto/Alamy), d (David Evans/National Geographic Image Collection), e (Bruce Dale/National Geographic Image Collection), 64 deer (Shutterstock), squirrel (Shutterstock), zebra (Shutterstock), elephant (Shutterstock), lion (Shutterstock), butterfly (Shutterstock), chameleon (Shutterstock), polar bear (Shutterstock), Arctic fox (Shutterstock), giraffe (Shutterstock), 65 (George F. Mobley/National Geographic Image Collection), 71 (Bryan Smith/National Geographic Image Collection), 72 ml (Geraint Lewis/Alamy), bl (Dreamworks SKG/The Kobal Collection), r (Egmont Publishing), 74 tl (Shutterstock), tr (Shutterstock), ml (Shutterstock), mr (Shutterstock), bl (Shutterstock), br (Shutterstock), 78 br (tony french/Alamy), b (Kevin Wheal/Alamy), 80 iPod (Neil Fraser/Alamy), vacuum cleaner (Shutterstock), wheel (Shutterstock), knife (Shutterstock), electrical circuit (Shutterstock), Sellotape (Shutterstock), fire (Shutterstock), internet (Dinodia Photos/Alamy), Morse code (Shutterstock), compass (Shutterstock), Marconi (World History Archive/Alamy), 81 (Cultura Creative/Alamy), 84 b (Signe Lansky), mr (Doug Lansky), 87 (Emory Kristof/National Geographic Image Collection), 88 tl (Terry Harris/Alamy), ml (Alex Zuccarelli/Alamy), 89 (Rachel Carbonell/Alamy), 91 (Shutterstock), 92 (NASA Archive/Alamy), 94 tl (Stocktrek Images/Getty Images), tr (Shutterstock), ul (Frans Lanting/National Geographic Image Collection), ur (Beverly Joubert/National Geographic Image Collection), ll (NASA/Corbis), lr (Shutterstock), b (Hemis/Alamy), br (Dean Conger /National Geographic Image Collection), 95 bl (© Red Bull Media House), b (Red Bull Media House), 96 (Antonio M. Rosario/The Image Bank/Getty Images), 97 (Paul Barton/Corbis)

Illustrations by: Peter Cornwell pp 12 l, 63, 69; James Gilleard (Folio Illustration) pp 22, 54, 58, 85; Matthew Hams pp 13, 20, 32, 35, 59, 77, 98; Alex Hedworth (Eye Candy Illustration) pp 12 tr, 63, 69; Dave Russell pp 6, 8, 16, 25, 36, 75, 92; Laszlo Veres (Beehive Illustration) pp 17, 19, 42, 67, 76, 78, 99

Printed in Greece by Bakis
1 2 3 4 5 6 7 8 9 10 – 17 16 15 14 13

Contents

Unit 1	People	Page 4
Unit 2	Possessions	Page 12
Unit 3	Places	Page 20
Unit 4	Free time	Page 28
Unit 5	Food	Page 36
Unit 6	Money	Page 44
Unit 7	Journeys	Page 52
Unit 8	Appearance	Page 60
Unit 9	Film and the arts	Page 68
Unit 10	Science	Page 76
Unit 11	Tourism	Page 84
Unit 12	The Earth	Page 92
IELTS test		Page 100
Audioscripts		Page 114
Answer key		Page 130

Unit 1 People

1a Interviewing people

Vocabulary personal information

1 Complete the first form (1–7) with these headings.

Address   Age   Country   First name   Job   Marital status
Surname

1	Helena	8
2	Lomakina	9
3	37	10
4	journalist	11
5	Russia	12
6	married	13
7	17a Arbat Street	14

2 Complete the second form (8–14) with your personal information.

Reading
new explorers

3 Complete these interviews with explorers with the questions (a–h).

a Are you the same age?
b Is your husband a scientist?
c Are you from the USA?
d Who is the other person in the photo?
e What's your job?
f Where are you now?
g Are your jobs the same?
h Where are you from?

4 🔊 **1.1** Listen and check your answers.

NEW EXPLORERS

This month we interviewed two new explorers. Our interviewer, Michelle Bright, telephoned them in the Galapagos Islands and Canada.

Tierney Thys
My name is Tierney Thys.

1 ....
   I'm from the state of California, but I'm not there at the moment.

2 ....
   I'm in the Galapagos Islands.

3 ....
   I'm a scientist.

4 ....
   No, he isn't. He's an engineer.

Grammar *be (am/is/are)*

5 🔊 **1.2** Choose the correct option to complete the interview. Then listen and check your answers.

I = Interviewer, J = Jon

I: ¹ *What are / What's* your name?
J: My ² *name am / name's* Jon Aanenson.
I: ³ *Is / Are* you from Norway?
J: Yes, ⁴ *I'm / I is* from the city of Bergen, but ⁵ *I'm not / I isn't* there at the moment.
I: Where ⁶ *is / are* you?
J: I'm in Greenland.
I: What ⁷ *is / are* your job?
J: I'm a scientist.
I: ⁸ *Are / Is* your wife a scientist?
J: No, she ⁹ *isn't / aren't*. She's a writer.

6 🔊 **1.3** Complete the interview with the correct form of *be*. Then listen and check your answers.

I = Interviewer, A = Ati

A: Hello, my name's Ati. I'm an archaeologist.
I: Where ¹ _____ you from?
A: Egypt.
I: ² _____ you there at the moment?
A: Yes, I ³ _____ here with my husband.
I: ⁴ _____ he an archaeologist?
A: Yes, he ⁵ _____, but he ⁶ _____ from Egypt. He's from England.
I: Are you the same age?
A: No, we ⁷ _____. I ⁸ _____ 35 and he's 38.

7 Put the words in order to make questions.

1 your   what's   name   ?

2 you   England   are   from   ?

3 you   how   old   are   ?

4 you   married   are   or   single?

5 student   you   are   a   ?

6 address   what   your   is   ?

8 Listen and respond asking and answering questions

🔊 **1.4** Listen to the questions in Exercise 7. Respond each time with answers for you.

> What's your name?   My name's …

9 Pronunciation contracted forms

🔊 **1.5** Listen to the verb *be* in these sentences. Do you hear the full form or the contracted form? Choose the correct option.

1 *What's / What is* your name?
2 He *isn't / is not* American.
3 *I'm / I am* from India.
4 *You're / You are* 28.
5 *I'm not / I am not* married.
6 We *aren't / are not* explorers.

Josh Thome (left)

My name's Josh Thome.

5 _____
He's Sol. We work together.

6 _____
No, we aren't. We're from Canada.

7 _____
No, we aren't. I'm thirty-six and Sol is thirty-five.

8 _____
Yes, they are. We're film-makers.

1b Families

Listening a family of gorillas

1 🎧 **1.6** Listen to a documentary about a family of gorillas. Number these topics in the correct order (1–3).

a the family _____
b daily life _____
c the location _____

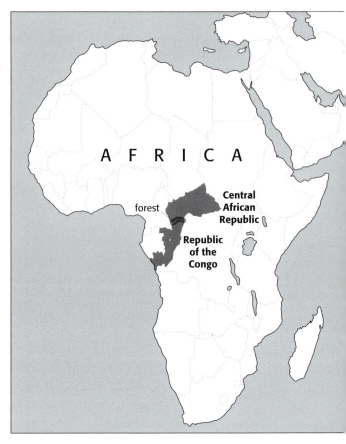

2 🎧 **1.6** Listen again. Choose the correct answer (a–c) for these questions.

1 Where are the forests?
 a in the Republic of the Congo
 b in the Central African Republic
 c between the Republic of the Congo and the Central African Republic

2 How many gorillas are in the region?
 a one hundred
 b thousands
 c hundreds

3 How old is Kingo?
 a 13
 b 30
 c 33

4 How many wives and children are in Kingo's family?
 a four
 b six
 c eight

5 When is the family together?
 a in the day
 b at night
 c all the time

3 Dictation Kingo's family

🎧 **1.7** Listen to part of the documentary again and complete the text.

Kingo's wives are Mama, Mekome, Beatrice and Ugly. Mekome is Kingo's favourite ¹_____ but Mama is the most important adult female gorilla. There are also four young gorillas, two ²_____ and two girls. Mama's ³_____ is Kusu. Mekome's son is Ekendy. Beatrice and Ugly are the girls' mothers. Their ⁴_____ are Gentil and Bomo.

The family is together all the time and they travel two kilometres a day. Kusu, Ekendy, Gentil and Bomo watch their ⁵_____ and mothers and they learn to find the fruit on different trees. After lunch, the ⁶_____ play with Kingo.

Unit 1 People

Vocabulary family

4 Complete the sentences about the family tree.

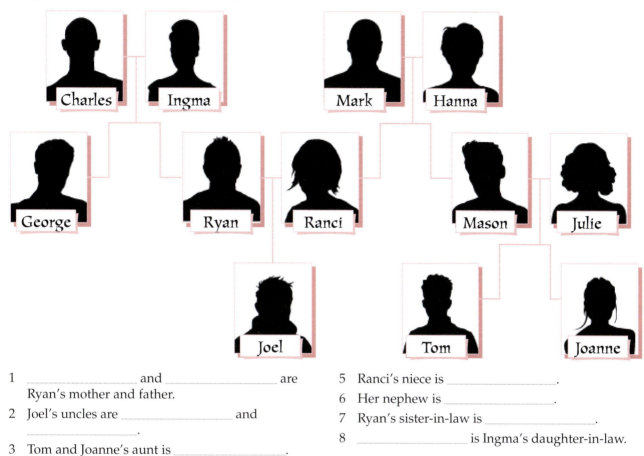

1 _____ and _____ are Ryan's mother and father.
2 Joel's uncles are _____ and _____.
3 Tom and Joanne's aunt is _____.
4 Ranci's brother-in-law is _____.
5 Ranci's niece is _____.
6 Her nephew is _____.
7 Ryan's sister-in-law is _____.
8 _____ is Ingma's daughter-in-law.

Grammar possessive 's and possessive adjectives

5 Complete what Ryan says about his family with these words.

he	her	it	their	our
's	my	they		

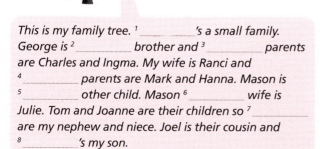

This is my family tree. ¹_____'s a small family. George is ²_____ brother and ³_____ parents are Charles and Ingma. My wife is Ranci and ⁴_____ parents are Mark and Hanna. Mason is ⁵_____ other child. Mason ⁶_____ wife is Julie. Tom and Joanne are their children so ⁷_____ are my nephew and niece. Joel is their cousin and ⁸_____'s my son.

6 Write a paragraph about your family.

7 Pronunciation the same or different sounds

🔊 1.8 Listen and complete the pairs of sentences.

1 a _____ in London.
  b _____ family is in London.
2 a _____ my brother.
  b _____ brother is a scientist.
3 a _____ you from Canada?
  b _____ family is from Canada.
4 a _____ eighteen.
  b _____ sister is eighteen.

7

1c Information about a country

Listening Malaysia

1 🔊 **1.9** Listen to some information about Malaysia. Tick the facts (1–8) you hear.

1 population ☐
2 jobs ☐
3 the capital city ☐
4 religion ☐
5 education ☐
6 languages ☐
7 mobile phones ☐
8 Internet ☐

2 🔊 **1.9** Listen again and complete the fact file.

Fact file: Malaysia

Malaysia has a population of ¹_____ million.

Kuala Lumpur is the capital city and there's a population of ²_____ million.

The average age is ³_____ years old.

There are a lot of different religions in Malaysia and ⁴_____% are Muslim.

Malay is the main language but many people also speak ⁵_____.

There are modern cities and beautiful countryside.

Over ⁶_____% of the population use the Internet.

Vocabulary everyday verbs

3 Match the sentence beginnings (1–5) with the endings (a–e).

1 They live
2 I have a
3 We work in an
4 90% of the population use the
5 The students speak

a office.
b Internet.
c in Australia.
d new mobile phone.
e English.

4 Complete these sentences about you.

1 I live in _____ .
2 I have _____ .
3 I work in _____ .
4 I use _____ .
5 I speak _____ .

Word focus *in*

5 Write *in* in these sentences.

1 They live ˄*in* the USA.
2 55% of the population work agriculture.
3 We live Dubai.
4 Amanda and Nigel work a shop.
5 49% of the people live the countryside.

Unit 1 People

1d At the conference

1 Pronunciation the alphabet

🔊 **1.10** Listen and repeat the seven letters.

A ...., ...,
B ...., ..., ..., ..., ...,
 ....,
F ...., ..., ..., ..., ...,
I ....
O
Q ...., ...
R

2 🔊 **1.11** Listen and match these letters with the same sound in Exercise 1.

C D E G H J K L M N P S
T U V W X Y Z

3 🔊 **1.12** Listen and check your answers in Exercise 2.

Real life meeting people for the first time

4 🔊 **1.13** Listen to people at a conference. Complete their name badges with their surname and country.

Name: Doctor T ....
Country: ....

Name: Beata ....
Country: ....

5 🔊 **1.13** Complete the conversation with these phrases. Then listen again and check.

| I'd like to introduce you | I'm from | my name's | nice talking to | nice to meet you |
| nice to meet you too | see you later | where are you from |

C: Hello, can I help you?
Z: Yes, I'm here for the conference.
C: What's your name?
Z: Doctor Zull. ¹........... Australia.
C: Zull. Zull. Zull. Is that Z-U-L-L?
Z: That's right.
C: Oh, here you are. Zull.
  ²..........., Doctor Zull. My name's Stella Williams. I'm the conference manager.
Z: ³............
C: So, here is some information about the conference. You're early so you can have a coffee over there. In fact, let me introduce you to someone. Beata?
P: Hello?

C: Beata, ⁴........... to Doctor Zull. He's also at the conference.
P: Nice to meet you.
  ⁵........... Beata Polit.
Z: Nice to meet you too, Beata. How do you spell your surname?
P: P-O-L-I-T
Z: So ⁶...........?
P: Poland. And you?
Z: Australia.
C: So, let me leave you both.
Z: OK. Thanks, Stella.
  ⁷........... you.
C: Yes. ⁸............
Z&P: Goodbye.

9

1e An introduction

1 Writing skill *and, but*

Complete the sentences with *and* or *but*.

1. I'm from Peru _____ I live in Chile.
2. Pedro and Alex are from Spain _____ they work in Madrid.
3. Sonia is at Oxford University _____ she isn't a student.
4. We're from Germany _____ we speak German and English.
5. I work in an office _____ from my home.
6. I have one sister _____ no brothers.

Writing an introduction

2 Read parts of six online introductions (1–6). Match them with the topics (a–f).

1
Hi! My name's Shefali and I'm twenty-five.

2
Hello. I'm Angie and I'm married with two daughters.

3
My family live in the countryside, but I live in the capital city.

4
Hello. I'm Monique. I'm from Belgium and I speak Dutch, French, German and English!

5
Hi! I'm Hanaka and I have three cats!

6
I'm Joseph and I'm a science teacher in a school in Kerala in southern India.

a age
b marital status and family
c job
d place you live
e language(s)
f other information

3 Read Brendan's plan for an online introduction. Write his introduction.

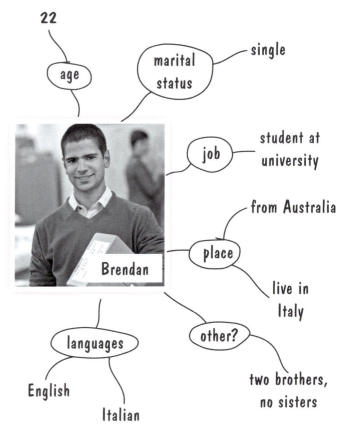

Hi! My name's Brendan and

Wordbuilding word roots

▶ **WORDBUILDING word roots**

When you learn a new word, you can sometimes make more words with the word. For example:

mother → grand**mother** → step**mother** → **mother**-in-law

photo → **phot**ograph → **phot**ographer

United → **United** Kingdom → **United** States of America → **United** Arab Emirates

1 Complete the sentences with these words or parts of words.

| grand | step | in-law |

1 My wife's mother is my **mother**-_____.
2 My _____ **mother** is the mother of my father.
3 My father's new wife is my _____ **mother**.

| first | middle | sur |

4 Is John your _____ **name** or your middle name?
5 Is your _____ **name** Smith or Jones?
6 Your name is John M. Grant. What's your _____ **name**?

| graph | grapher |

7 My uncle is a **photo**_____.
8 This **photo**_____ is of my husband and me.

| brother | father | sister |

9 My **step**_____ is from my father's first marriage. She's thirteen.
10 Is your **step**_____ your father's or your mother's son?
11 How old is your **step**_____? Is he 50?

Learning skills write a personal sentence

2 When you learn a new word, write it in a sentence about you. It helps you remember the new word. Compare these sentences by different students using the word *parent*.
1 My grandparents live with my parents.
2 I'm a parent with three children.
3 I have one parent. I live with my mother. My father is dead.

3 Look at these words from Unit 1. Write sentences for you with each word.
1 name
2 wife
3 single
4 cousin
5 population
6 live
7 speak

Check!

4 Complete the crossword. Find the answers in Unit 1 of the Student's Book.

Across

4 A lot of people work in _____ in the countryside.
5 1,000,000 is a _____.
7 The Majlis al Jinn Cave is in _____.
8 Mike and Sally Burney are _____.

Down

1 Maeve Leakey is Louise Leakey's _____.
2 A _____ is 1,000,000,000 in the USA and 1,000,000,000,000 in the UK.
3 The Leakey family live in _____ Africa.
6 The sister of your nephew is your _____.

Unit 2 Possessions

2a Possessions

1 Vocabulary extra colours

What colour are the flags? Use these words.

| blue + yellow | yellow + black | red + yellow |
| white + black | | |

1 Germany: black, _____ and _____

2 United Arab Emirates: red, green, _____ and _____

3 Jamaica: _____, green and _____

4 Sweden: _____ and _____

2 What colours are on your country's flag?

Vocabulary everyday objects

3 Match the explorer's possessions (1–10) with the words.

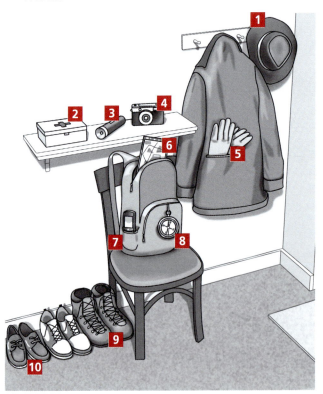

hat _____	mobile phone _____
shoes _____	first-aid kit _____
boots _____	torch _____
compass _____	gloves _____
map _____	camera _____

Reading information for visitors

4 Complete the information leaflet for visitors to a national park. Use words from Exercise 3.

Welcome to Canyonlands National Park

Information for visitors

We want all visitors to our beautiful park to have a great experience. Please read this safety information at the beginning of your visit.

- The weather can change quickly in the park. When it's cold, you lose 80% of your body's heat from your head. Take a ^{1}_____ with you and wear it when you are cold.

- You can get medical help at the National Park visitor's centre, but take a ^{2}_____ with you on long walks.

- For long walks and climbing, you can buy a ^{3}_____ from the National Park shop. This shows all the walks and routes through the park.

- There are three levels of routes for walkers and climbers in the park: green is easy, orange is difficult, red is very difficult. On green routes you can wear training ^{4}_____, but on orange and red routes, wear strong walking ^{5}_____.

Grammar plural nouns

5 🔊 **1.14** Choose the correct option to complete the conversation. Then listen and check.

I = Interviewer, C = Climber

I: Is this your [1] *rucksack / rucksacks*?
C: Yes, it is. And these are [2] *map / maps* for my next climb.
I: Is this a [3] *first-aid kit / first-aid kits*?
C: Yes, it's very important. And also this torch. In fact, there are two [4] *torch / torches* in my rucksack, and a [5] *compass / compasses*.
I: Where is your next climb?
C: In the Himalayas. It's cold there and these are my [6] *glove / gloves*. And this is a good [7] *hat / hats*.
I: Are these your [8] *boot / boots*?
C: Yes, they are.

> ▶ **SPELL CHECK plural nouns**
> - Add *-s* to most nouns: *boot* → *boots*, *shoe* → *shoes*
> - Add *-es* to nouns ending in *-ch, -o, -s, -ss, -sh* and *-x*: *compass* → *compasses*
> - Change nouns ending in *-f* (or *-fe*) to *-ves*: *shelf* → *shelves*
> - Change nouns ending in *-y* after a consonant to *-ies*: *country* → *countries*
> - Don't change the *-y* to an *-i* after a vowel: *holiday* → *holidays*
> - Some nouns are irregular: *woman* → *women*, *child* → *children*

6 Look at the spell check box. Write the plural form of these nouns.

1 mobile phone ....
2 person ....
3 box ....
4 torch ....
5 knife ....
6 city ....
7 camera ....
8 man ....
9 key ....

7 Pronunciation /s/, /z/ or /ɪz/

a 🔊 **1.15** Listen to the pronunciation of *-s* at the end of these plural nouns. Complete the table with the nouns.

| boots | boxes | cities | compasses | hats |
| keys | knives | maps | mobile phones | |

/s/	/z/	/ɪz/

b 🔊 **1.15** Listen again and repeat.

Grammar *this*, *that*, *these*, *those*

8 Look at the pictures and complete the questions. Use *this*, *that*, *these* or *those* and a singular or plural noun.

1 Are ___*those*___ your ___*gloves*___ ?
2 Is _____ your _____ ?
3 Are _____ your _____ ?
4 Is _____ your _____ ?

2b A place to stay

Listening and reading the Jumbo hostel

1 🎧 1.16 Listen to and read the article about the Jumbo hostel. Complete the text with the missing numbers.

The Jumbo hostel

About [1]_____ million passengers use Stockholm-Arlanda airport every year. Aeroplanes take off and land all the time, but at the side of the runway there's a big Boeing [2]_____ aeroplane and it never takes off. That's because it's a hostel called 'Jumbo Stay'. It's only [3]_____ minutes on foot from the main airport terminal or [4]_____ minutes by bus.

The Jumbo Stay is a real aeroplane from [5]_____ and from the outside you think it's a normal aeroplane. But on the inside it's very different.

There's a reception desk and a [6]_____-hour-a-day café in the old first-class seating area.

There aren't any aeroplane seats. There are [7]_____ rooms with [8]_____ beds. Each room has one or [9]_____ beds, a TV and the Internet. The rooms are small but cheap and visitors usually only stay for a night. You can also sleep in the cockpit of the aeroplane. It's more expensive but it's a private double room with a shower. Jumbo Stay is very popular with families and with travellers who want a different kind of travel experience.

2 Read the article again. Are the sentences true (T) or false (F)?

1 Stockholm-Arlanda is a busy airport.
2 People fly in Jumbo Stay.
3 It's a long distance from the airport to the hostel.
4 There's a café on the aeroplane.
5 There aren't any aeroplane seats in Jumbo Stay.
6 There is one bed in every room.
7 People often stay for a week.
8 You can sleep in the cockpit.

3 Match these words from the article with the definitions (1–8).

| hostel | on foot | runway | double |
| cheap | cockpit | expensive | take off |

1 _____ (v): to leave the ground in a plane
2 _____ (n): a road for aeroplanes at an airport
3 _____ (n): a type of hotel, and people often stay in rooms with other visitors
4 _____ (adv): by walking
5 _____ (adj): not cost a lot of money
6 _____ (n): the front of the aeroplane, normally for the pilot
7 _____ (adj): cost a lot of money
8 _____ (adj): a room for two people

Grammar *there is/are*, prepositions of place

4 A visitor is at the reception of Jumbo Stay. Complete the conversation with *is*, *are*, *isn't* or *aren't*.

R = Receptionist, V = Visitor
R: Hello, can I help you?
V: Yes, ¹_____ there any rooms tonight?
R: There ²_____ any double rooms, but there ³_____ a single room.
V: ⁴_____ there a desk in the room? I need to work on my laptop.
R: No, there ⁵_____, but there is a small table and chair. And there ⁶_____ large tables in our café. Lots of people use those. The café is open 24 hours a day.
V: And ⁷_____ there Internet in the café?
R: Yes, there ⁸_____.
V: Sounds perfect.

5 Complete the sentences with these words.

| above | next | on | left | the right |
| under | | | | |

1 There is a picture _____ the wall.
2 The chair is _____ to the table.
3 The bed is on _____.
4 The windows are on the _____.
5 There is a light _____ your bed.
6 A carpet is _____ the table.

Vocabulary furniture

6 Complete the word puzzle with the names of the furniture. What's the mystery word?

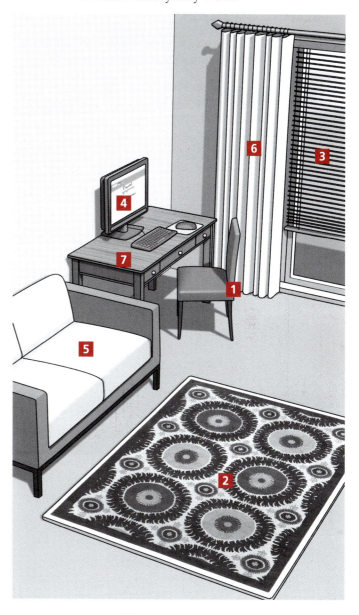

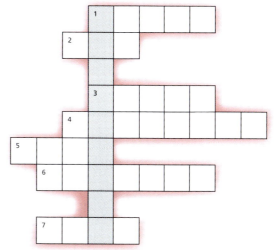

Mystery word: _____

2c A global company

Listening IKEA

1 🔘 **1.17** Listen to a radio programme about IKEA. Number these pictures in the correct order (1–4).

a

b

c

d

2 Dictation IKEA

🔘 **1.17** Listen again and complete the text.

IKEA is a ¹_____ company with IKEA shops all over the world. There are ²_____ IKEA shops in ³_____ different countries. Over ⁴_____ people shop at IKEA every year.

The company is famous for ⁵_____ and products for the home. You can buy ⁶_____, _____, _____, kitchen ⁷_____ and office ⁸_____. It sells more than 10,000 different items.

IKEA furniture is often made in ⁹_____ but company products are from 50 different countries. For example, one factory in ¹⁰_____ makes 30 million tables, desks and wardrobes a year.

IKEA also has other services. There are ¹¹_____ in the shops and the food is Swedish. There is an IKEA mobile phone service in the ¹²_____. And in some countries you can even buy a house from IKEA.

Vocabulary countries and nationalities

3 Make sentences about the companies and their countries.

1 Burberry / Britain
   Burberry is a British company.
2 BMW / Germany
3 Gucci / Italy
4 Sony / Japan
5 Petrobas / Brazil
6 Inditex / Spain
7 Alcatel-Lucent / France
8 Google / USA

4 Pronunciation word stress

a Match these countries with the stress patterns.

Brazil	Canada	England	France
Germany	Greece	Italy	Japan	Peru
Poland	Spain	Sweden		

1 ●   *France*
2 ●●
3 ●●
4 ●●●

b 🔘 **1.18** Listen and check your answers.

16

2d At the shop

Real life shopping

1 🔊 **1.19** Listen to three conversation in different shops. Tick what the customer buys each time.

Conversation 1

Conversation 2

Conversation 3

2 🔊 **1.19** Match the questions and sentences (1–5) with the responses (a–e). Then listen again and check.

1 Yes, I'd like a hat, please.
2 How much is it?
3 I'd like a bag, please.
4 Are they all the same?
5 Milk and sugar?

a Fifteen pounds.
b No, this one is ten dollars and this one is ten dollars fifty.
c Which one?
d Just milk, please. No sugar.
e Which size?

3 Listen and respond saying which one

🔊 **1.20** You are a customer in the three shops in Exercise 1. Listen to the shop assistant and respond each time. Choose the item you want in each shop.

> Hello, can I help you?

> Yes, I'd like a hat, please.

Word focus *one/ones*

4 Look at the pictures and complete the conversations between a customer (C) and a shop assistant (A).

Conversation 1

C: I'd like this ¹ _____T-shirt_____, please.
A: Which ² _____one_____ ?
C: The ³ _____black one_____.

Conversation 2

C: I'd like this bottle of ⁴ _____, please.
A: Which ⁵ _____ ?
C: The ⁶ _____.

Conversation 3

C: I'd like these ⁷ _____, please.
A: Which ⁸ _____ ?
C: The ⁹ _____.

5 Pronunciation contrastive stress

a 🔊 **1.21** Listen and underline the two stressed words in each sentence.

1 This one is nice but that one is perfect!
2 These ones are bad but those ones are good.
3 This one is medium but that one is large.
4 These ones are seven pounds but those ones are five.

b 🔊 **1.21** Listen again and repeat.

2e Advertisements

Vocabulary adjectives

1 These photographs show opposites. Match the adjectives with the photos.

cheap expensive fast large modern
old slow small useful useless

1 ……………… ………………

2 ……………… ………………

3 ……………… ………………

4 ……………… ………………

5 ……………… ………………

2 Writing skill describing objects with adjectives

Read the comments and complete the descriptions.

1 'I love your green bag! Is it new?'
a *new, green* bag
2 'This motorbike is Japanese. It's very fast.'
a ……………… motorbike
3 'There's a white table for sale but it's small.'
a ……………… table
4 'The painting is Italian. It's very old.'
an ……………… painting
5 'This kitchen knife is very useful. It's French, I think.'
a ……………… kitchen knife
6 'I like this blue rucksack. It's very strong.'
a ……………… rucksack

Writing advertisements

3 Write three 'for sale' adverts for these objects.

BUY NOW!

………………
………………
………………
………………
………………

FOR SALE

………………
………………
………………
………………
………………

SALE!

………………
………………
………………
………………
………………

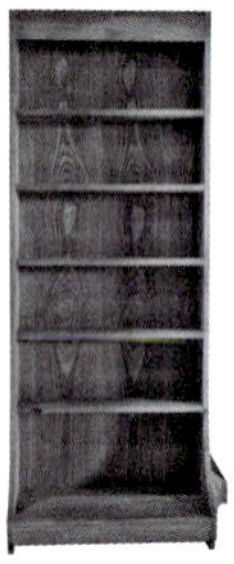

Unit 2 Possessions

Wordbuilding suffixes (1)

▶ **WORDBUILDING suffixes (1)**

We add suffixes to words and make new words.
For example:

verb → noun: *teach* → *teacher*

noun → adjective: *England* → *English*

- We add *-er* to talk about people and their job or activity: *teacher*
- We often add *-ist* to talk about people and musical instruments: *guitarist*
- We add *-ish*, *-n*, *-an*, *-ian* or *-ese* to talk about nationalities: *English*, *German*, *Romanian*, *Japanese*

1 Choose the correct option to complete these sentences.

1. I'm an office *work / worker*.
2. My aunt is a music *teach / teacher*.
3. I love the *saxophone / saxophonist*. It's a great musical instrument.
4. This car is made in *Brazil / Brazilian*.
5. He's my favourite *guitar / guitarist*.
6. I like *Vietnam / Vietnamese* food.
7. This is Mozart's *piano / pianist*. It's beautiful.
8. The *Spain / Spanish* team won the football match.

2 Complete the words with these suffixes.

-r	-n	-an	-er	-ian	-ese	-ish
-ist						

1. I learn Engl_____ at night school.
2. She's America_____.
3. Who is the pian_____? Is she famous?
4. J K Rowling is a children's write_____.
5. Berlin is a Germ_____ city.
6. There's a very good Middle Eastern restaurant in town. I love Leban_____ food.
7. Gucci is an Ital_____ fashion company.
8. Who is your favourite sing_____?

Learning skills names on objects

3 Stick on objects in your house their name in English. Mark the word stress and test yourself every day.

4 Copy these labels and stick them to objects in your house. Use your dictionary to help you.

Check!

5 Put the letters of these anagrams in order to make words from Unit 2 of the Student's Book. (The clues in brackets will help.)

1. SOPSESSION (this object is yours)
   possession
2. BLICMER (Andy Torbet is this)
   _____
3. FRUNIRUTE (e.g. a sofa, a chair, a desk)
   _____
4. CHUTD (the nationality of the people in the Netherlands) _____
5. NIMI (a famous car) _____

Unit 3 Places

3a City life

Vocabulary telling the time

1 Match the clocks with the times (1–8).

1 It's three o'clock.
2 It's quarter past three.
3 It's half past three.
4 It's twenty-five minutes past three.
5 It's twenty-five minutes to three.
6 It's five minutes past three.
7 It's five minutes to three.
8 It's quarter to three.

2 Write the times.

1 5.00   *It's five o'clock.*
2 7.05
3 9.15
4 1.25
5 4.30
6 3.35
7 8.45
8 10.55

Listening the time in different places

3 1.22 Listen and number the places in order (1–4).

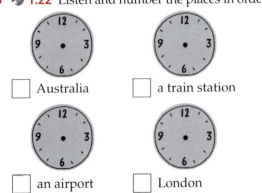

☐ Australia   ☐ a train station
☐ an airport   ☐ London

4 1.22 Listen again and draw the time on the clocks.

City of the future

Songdo is a big city. It's over six km² and is on an artificial island in South Korea. But the streets of Songdo are very quiet and the air is clean because there are only one or two cars. The roofs of houses and offices are beautiful because there are plants and gardens. So why isn't this modern city crowded with people? Why isn't there a lot of traffic and air pollution? At the moment only 22,000 people live in Songdo, but about 65,000 people plan to live here in the future. That's because Songdo is a new and very 'intelligent' city. It's only ten years old and has state-of-the-art technology. For example, the Internet is in everything: in people's homes, their cars and in the roads.

At the centre of the city is a 'control centre'. It receives information from the Internet about buildings, traffic and the weather. With this information, the control centre can 'change' the city. For example, if there aren't people on a street at night, the control centre can switch the street lights off. If there are a lot of cars on one street, drivers receive information from the control centre.

Songdo is called a 'smart city' and its architects think it is the city of the future.

Glossary
architect (n) /ˈɑːkɪˌtekt/ a person who designs buildings and cities
artificial (adj) /ˌɑːtɪˈfɪʃl/ not real or natural, made by humans
control centre (n) /kənˈtrəʊlˌsentə/ a place which manages everything
smart (adj) /smɑːt/ very intelligent
state-of-the-art (adj) /ˌsteɪtəvðəˈɑːt/ the most modern

Reading a city

5 Read the article about Songdo. Answer the questions with *Yes, No* or *Don't know* (because the information isn't in the article).

1. Is there a lot of traffic in Songdo?
2. Are there plants on the top of buildings?
3. Are there popular shopping areas in Songdo?
4. Are there any old parts of the city?
5. Is the Internet important in the city?
6. Are there people in the control centre?
7. Do car drivers send information to the control centre?
8. Do people like living in Songdo?

Vocabulary adjectives about cities

6 Write the opposites of these adjectives. Find the answers in the article about Songdo.

1. small
2. noisy
3. dirty
4. ugly
5. old (x2)
6. uncrowded
7. stupid

7 Read these comments about cities and places. Match an adjective from Exercise 6 with each comment.

1. 'Only a 1,000 people live here.'
2. 'They never clean the streets.'
3. 'We don't like looking at the new office building in the middle of the city.'
4. 'I always go shopping on Tuesdays because there aren't many people.'
5. 'This part of the city is from the fifteenth century.'

Grammar present simple (*I/you/we/they*)

8 Complete the sentences with the affirmative or negative form of these verbs.

eat	go	have	like	live	meet
study	work				

1. I _____ to work at half past eight every morning.
2. I _____ a car so I go to work on the bus.
3. They shop online because they _____ shopping in the city. It's very crowded.
4. I _____ in that office building over there.
5. We _____ at the university in Berlin. It's a great city!
6. We _____ in cafés at lunchtime because they are very expensive.
7. They _____ friends here in the evenings because the food is very good.
8. Most people _____ in the city centre because it's very polluted. They are in the suburbs.

Glossary
suburbs (n) /ˈsʌbɜːbz/ area of houses not in the city centre

Grammar present simple questions

9 Use the prompts to write questions for these answers.

1. what / do ?
   What do you do?
   I'm a student at the university.
2. where / live ?

   In Singapore.
3. do / go to work by car ?

   No, I don't. I go by bicycle.
4. what time / eat lunch ?

   At midday.
5. like shopping ?

   Yes, I do. With friends.

10 Listen and respond questions about your life

🔊 **1.23** Listen to the questions in Exercise 9 and respond with an answer for you.

21

3b Places of work

1 Vocabulary extra jobs

Write the job.

a ....

b ....

c ....

d ....

e ....

f ....

g ....

h ....

Listening talking about work

2 🔊 **1.24** Listen to eight people. Match each person with a job (a–h) from Exercise 1.

Person 1 ....
Person 2 ....
Person 3 ....
Person 4 ....
Person 5 ....
Person 6 ....
Person 7 ....
Person 8 ....

Vocabulary places of work

3 🔊 **1.24** Complete the places of work, then listen again and check your answers.

1 Photographer: 'I have a s................, but a lot of my photos are of animals in different places.'
2 Doctor: 'I work in the centre of the city in a h................'
3 Waiter: 'I also work in an expensive r................ in the centre of Paris at night.'
4 Sailor: 'I spend more time on the b................ than in my house.'
5 Accountant: 'I work for a large firm in an o................ b................'
6 Student: 'My classes are three days a week so I go to the u................ on Mondays, Wednesdays and Thursdays.'
7 Pilot: 'I arrive at the a................ early because I fly from London to New York.'
8 Teacher: 'I don't work in a normal c................. I have an office and I teach my students through my computer and the Internet.'

Reading where you work

4 Read the article. Are these sentences true (T) or false (F)?

1 We don't often understand the importance of a workplace.
2 It's a bad idea to put your desk next to a window.
3 It's difficult to find a comfortable office chair.
4 Spend more money on a good chair.
5 Plants and lamps are a good idea and they aren't expensive.
6 Clean your desk at the beginning of the working day.

Improve your workplace

Is your place of work a good place to work? Lots of people don't understand how their place of work can affect their work. Here are some simple ideas.

- Put your desk near a window because natural light makes people feel better. And you can enjoy a nice view.
- Is your chair comfortable? This is very important for people in offices with desks. Nowadays, a lot of designers make modern chairs for people who use computers a lot. Sometimes they are more expensive, but they're a good idea.
- Plants are a cheap way to improve the office. They make office life nicer and scientists say plants make us happy at work. Lighting also makes a big difference and you don't have to spend a lot on good lamps.
- At the end of every day, tidy your desk. Put your books and papers away on the shelf so everything is ready for tomorrow.

Word focus *work*

5 Complete the sentences with *for* or *with*.

1 There are ten people in my office and I work _____ all of them. We're a team!
2 I work _____ a large company in the United States. It's a good job.
3 They work _____ their father. He's the boss.
4 Do you work _____ a group of people?

Grammar present simple (*he/she/it*)

6 Complete the article with the correct form of these verbs.

| come | go | like | not spend | work |
| not work | sail | study | | |

Brad Mardell ¹_____ from New Zealand and he's a marine biologist. He ²_____ in an office at his university, but he ³_____ a lot of time there. He ⁴_____ being under the water because he ⁵_____ animals in the sea. Brad is married and his wife, Gina, ⁶_____ with him on expeditions. But she ⁷_____ under the water because she ⁸_____ the boat. 'We're a good team,' says Brad.

7 Complete these questions about the article.

1 Where _____ ?
   New Zealand.
2 Where _____ ?
   In an office.
3 Does _____ a lot of time there?
   No, he doesn't.
4 Does _____ under the water?
   Yes, he does.
5 What _____ ?
   Animals in the sea.
6 _____ Gina _____ with him on expeditions?
   Yes, she does.
7 _____ she _____ under the water?
   No, because she sails the boat.

8 Pronunciation *-s* endings

🎵 **1.25** Listen to the *-s* endings in these verbs. Complete the table with the verbs.

| comes | dances | finishes | goes | likes |
| spends | starts | teaches | works | |

/s/	/z/	/ɪz/

3c Languages

Listening places and languages

1 🎵 **1.26** Listen to three parts of a lecture about languages. Match the parts with the charts (A–C).

Part 1: _____   Part 2: _____   Part 3: _____

A

Top five languages on the Internet

- English — 540 million users
- Chinese — (1) _____ million
- Spanish — (2) _____ million
- Japanese — 100 million
- Portuguese — (3) _____ million

B

Speakers of English in the world

7%   (4) _____ %   (5) _____ %

Native | Non-native speakers | Non-speakers

C

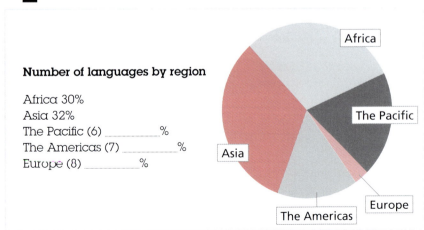

Number of languages by region

Africa 30%
Asia 32%
The Pacific (6) _____ %
The Americas (7) _____ %
Europe (8) _____ %

2 🎵 **1.26** Listen again. Complete the charts with the missing numbers.

Vocabulary cardinal and ordinal numbers

3 Complete the sentences with these numbers. Write the numbers as words.

| 1st | 2 | 3rd | 5 | 6 |
| 7̶ | 20 | 100th | | |

1 Ten, nine, eight, _seven_, six, _____, four, three, _____, one!
2 New Year's Day is on the _____ of January.
3 Three and three is _____.
4 There are three daughters in my family and I'm the _____.
5 This book costs _____-five dollars.
6 You are our _____ customer!

4 Pronunciation saying numbers

a 🎵 **1.27** Listen to these sentences. Tick the number you hear.

1 13   30
2 5th 15th
3 66   166
4 3rd 33rd
5 18   80

b 🎵 **1.28** Listen and repeat both numbers.

3d In a new city

Vocabulary places in a city

1 Read these comments from different tourists in a city. Which places do they talk about?

aquarium	hotel	library	museum	park
car park	theatre	tourist information centre		

1 'I need information about the city.'
   tourist information centre
2 'Where can I learn about the history of this city?'
3 'Let's relax outside on the grass.'
4 'Where can we leave the car?'
5 'This is an old building. It's full of books!'
6 'What's on tonight? Is there a play or a musical?'
7 'I need a room for the night.'
8 'Let's go here. The children love looking at sea life.'

Real life giving directions

2 🔊 **1.29** Listen to a tourist asking for directions to three places. In each conversation, where does the tourist want to go?

1 _____
2 _____
3 _____

3 🔊 **1.29** Listen again and tick the correct place (A, B or C) on each map. The tourist is on X.

1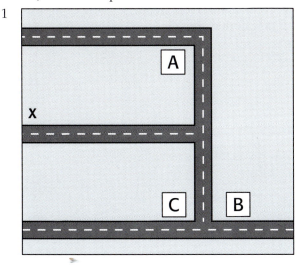

2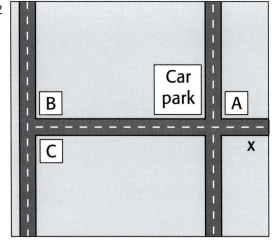

3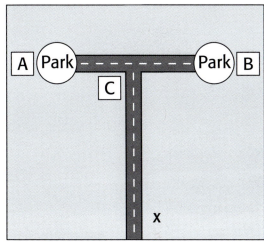

4 🔊 **1.29** Complete the conversations. Then listen again and check.

T = Tourist, L = Local person

1 T: Excuse me. I need a bank. Is there one ¹_____ here?
   L: Yes, it's near. Go ²_____ up this street and take the first street on the right. Then ³_____ left and it's there.

2 T: Hello. ⁴_____ is the theatre? The play starts in ten minutes.
   L: That's OK. It's about two minutes ⁵_____. Go across this road and go ⁶_____ a car park on your right. Then ⁷_____ the first street on the left. It's on the corner.

3 T: Hello. Is the tourist information centre near ⁸_____?
   L: Err, it's about ten minutes away. ⁹_____ straight up this street and turn left at the end. Go ¹⁰_____ a small park and the information centre is on the other side of it.

3e Describing a place

Travel Guide FEATURES | TRIP PLANNER | ACTIVITIES | HOTELS | SEARCH

Maui

Andrew McCarthy is a writer for a travel magazine. He describes his favourite places on the Hawaiian island of Maui.

¹ _____. It has beautiful sand and a view of the West Maui Mountains. In the evening, the sun sets in front of you.

² _____. Marisa Samuels makes a great lunch on the island. Buy the chicken kebab and eat it under the kiawe tree.

³ _____. So for a good cup of coffee, go to Grandma's Coffee House. Sit outside and talk to the local people.

⁴ _____. It's a hard walk but there's the Haleakalā volcano and it has a great view of the Pacific Ocean.

⁵ _____. There are no electric lights so, at night, watch the Moon.

1 Writing skill capital letters

Each sentence needs one capital letter. Circle the mistake and rewrite the word.

1 I live in the city of (k)arachi.   *Karachi*
2 Let me introduce you to my husband george.
3 I speak three languages and french is my favourite.
4 Is it monday today?
5 In the USA, july 4th is an important day.
6 this is a beautiful city in the south of the country.
7 It's cold in the winter but i love this time of year.
8 I love travelling with just a backpack in morocco.
9 He has a small house and his address is 21 haversham Street.
10 Mr grant comes from the next town to me.

Writing a travel website

2 Complete the description of Maui with these sentences (a–e).

a I love a good cup of coffee in the morning.
b The best place to eat is Makena Grill.
c My favourite beach is Keawakapu Beach.
d Stay at a cabin near Haleakala volcano.
e My favourite walk is in the Polipoli Spring State Recreation Area.

3 Think about your favourite place. Complete this description about it.

My favourite place is _____

My favourite café/restaurant is _____

My favourite walk is _____

Wordbuilding collocations

▶ **WORDBUILDING collocations**

A collocation is a combination of words that happens very often. A lot of nouns have adjective and noun collocations:

large city (adjective + noun)

capital city (noun + noun)

1 Match these nouns with the groups of words (1–8).

centre	hotel	language	office
park	time	transport	work

1 first / foreign / official
2 five-star / comfortable / friendly
3 car / local / wildlife
4 head / small / government
5 boarding / good / closing
6 city / town / shopping
7 public / private / air
8 full-time / office / hard

2 Complete these sentences with words from Exercise 1.

1 English is my _____ language. All my family is from the UK.
2 This is a _____ hotel. A family owns it and everyone says 'Hello'.
3 Let's visit this _____ park. There are some beautiful animals here.
4 The _____ office for our company is in Atlanta.
5 This shop's _____ time is at six o'clock.
6 You can buy everything you need at this _____ centre.
7 The _____ transport system is very good in this city. There are a lot of trains and buses.
8 I don't like _____ work. I want a job outside.

Learning skills test a friend

3 Learning English with friends is useful and more fun! For example, choose five new words from today's English lesson. Write five sentences with the words. Read them to your partner but don't say the word. Say *beep* instead. Your partner guesses the missing word.

English is my BEEP language.

Second?

Correct! English is my second language.

Check!

4 Answer these questions with the name of a country or city. Then check your answers in Unit 3 of the Student's Book.

1 Where is the Midnight Sun Restaurant?
   N_____
2 Which city in Japan has crowded shopping centres but areas with no cars?
   T_____
3 Which city in Colombia was polluted in the past but now the air is clean?
   B_____
4 Which city has Centennial Olympic Park?
   A_____
5 Which country has the number one language in the world?   C_____
6 Which islands have 109 languages?
   V_____
7 Where is the language of Amurdag from?
   A_____
8 Which city has Krasnaya Presnaya Park?
   M_____

Unit 4 Free time

4a In your free time

Vocabulary and listening
free-time activities

1 Match these verbs to the pictures and write the names of the activities.

go   play   do   play   watch
play   go to   meet

1   *play a musical instrument*

2   _____

3   _____

4   _____

5   _____

6   _____

7   _____

8   _____

Listening at a sports centre

2   1.30   Listen to an interview with a customer at a sports centre. Tick her answers on the questionnaire.

Get Fit Sports Centre

As part of our customer service, we would like to know how you use the Get Fit Sports Centre. Please tick the answers for you and write more information.

1   Do you play team sports (e.g. football, hockey)? ☐
   _____

2   Do you do martial arts (e.g. Tae Kwon Do, Judo)? ☐
   _____

3   Do you go to the gym? ☐
   _____

4   Do you watch the training videos on our website? ☐
   _____

5   Do you meet friends in the café? ☐
   _____

3 🔊 **1.30** Complete the interview (1–5) with these phrases (a–e). Then listen again and check.
a It's really good for me.
b It's relaxing.
c that isn't a team sport
d It's fun.
e They're really useful.

I = Interviewer, C = Customer

I: Hello, I work for the sports centre and we'd like to know more about our customers. Can I ask you some questions about your free time?
C: Sure.
I: Great. OK. So, first of all, do you play team sports at the sports centre?
C: Well, I play tennis. But ¹_____. Err, so the answer is no.
I: OK. And what about martial arts? You know, like Tae Kwon Do or Judo.
C: Yes, I do Judo on Tuesday evenings. I really like it. ²_____
I: OK. That's good. And do you go to the gym?
C: Yes. That's the main reason I come here. ³_____
I: I see. And on our website we have training videos. Do you ever watch them?
C: No, I don't. What are they?
I: We made some videos about exercise and how you can do more exercise at home as well as in the gym. ⁴_____
C: Right. Sounds interesting.
I: And my last question. Do you meet friends in the café?
C: Yes, sometimes. I go to the gym with friends and sometimes we have a coffee in the café afterwards. ⁵_____
I: So the answer is yes. OK. Thanks. That's everything.

Grammar *like/love* + *-ing*

> ▶ **SPELL CHECK** *-ing*
> • Add *-ing* to most verbs: *play* → *playing*
> • For verbs ending in *-e*, delete the *-e*: *dance* → *dancing*
> • Double the final consonant in some verbs ending with a vowel and a consonant: *shop* → *shopping*

4 Look at the spell check box. Then write the *-ing* form of these verbs.
1 swim _____
2 sing _____
3 live _____
4 go _____
5 run _____
6 watch _____
7 fish _____
8 cycle _____

5 Pronunciation /ŋ/

🔊 **1.31** Listen and repeat the answers in Exercise 4.

6 Rewrite these sentences using the verbs in brackets.
1 We like music. (listen to)
   We like listening to music.
2 Bob likes tennis. (play)
   _____
3 I love languages. (learn)
   _____
4 They like football. (watch)
   _____
5 Do you like the gym? (go to)
   _____
6 My brother doesn't like nightclubs. (dance at)
   _____
7 The twins don't like homework. (do)
   _____
8 We like foreign food. (eat)
   _____

7 Listen and respond talking about your likes and dislikes

🔊 **1.32** Listen to four questions about free time. Say your answers and then compare your answers with the model answers that follow.

Do you like swimming?

Yes, I do. It's relaxing and it's good for me.

4b Free time at work

Reading explorers and their free time

1 Read the article. Match the explorers (A–D) with these sentences.

1 This explorer works underwater.
2 This explorer studies the stars in space.
3 This explorer takes photographs of nature.
4 This explorer has an office in two countries.

What do you do in your free time?

National Geographic explorers are busy people. They travel all over the world and they are never bored at work. So what do they do in their free time? We ask four of them.

A Tshewang Wangchuk
Tshewang Wangchuk is a conservationist.

He works with nature and helps areas with mountains, rivers and animals. He has an office in Washington DC and in Thimphu, Bhutan. When he travels, he always takes a good book with him. He likes cycling when he has time and he enjoys listening to and playing music. At the weekend he spends time with his wife and children. He says, 'When you enjoy your work, you don't need separate free time.'

C Shannon Switzer
Shannon Switzer is a photographer and journalist.

She loves the outdoors and so a lot of her photography is in mountains or on the ocean. She is also interested in the conservation of water. She works in an office, but she doesn't often stay inside all day. For example, she likes riding horses and surfing. And at home, she says, 'I love spending time with family, playing games and eating big meals together.'

B Knicole Colón
Knicole Colón is an astronomer.

She sometimes goes to observatories and looks at space through a telescope. But she usually goes to her office and studies information about space and stars. In her free time she likes watching a good movie or playing computer games. But she also likes 'doing nothing'.

D Michael Lombardi
Michael Lombardi is a writer and underwater explorer.

He loves the ocean and he often goes diving. He writes about his expeditions, nature and the environment. Michael often writes about the sea. He doesn't have much free time but he says, 'I do my best to live a healthy lifestyle. I eat well, do exercise and spend time with family.'

2 Read the article again. What do the explorers do in their free time? Tick the activities.

		A Tshewang Wangchuk	B Knicole Colón	C Shannon Switzer	D Michael Lombardi
1	reading books	✓			
2	watching a film				
3	listening to music				
4	playing a musical instrument				
5	cycling				
6	riding horses				
7	playing games or computer games				
8	spending time with family				
9	surfing				

Grammar adverbs of frequency, expressions of frequency

3 Complete these sentences from the article in Exercise 1 with adverbs of frequency.

1 They are _____ bored at work.
2 When he travels, he _____ takes a good book with him.
3 She _____ goes to observatories and looks at space through a telescope.
4 But she _____ goes to her office and studies information about space and stars.
5 She does _____ stay inside all day.
6 He loves the ocean and he _____ goes diving.

4 Rewrite the sentences using an adverb of frequency.

1 I read a book <u>two or three nights a week</u> before I go to bed.
   I often read a book before I go to bed.
2 I go to work <u>every day</u> at eight.

3 I meet my family <u>once a year</u>.

4 I go clothes shopping <u>once or twice a month</u>.

5 I'm busy <u>all the time</u>.

6 At work, I <u>don't</u> take lunch breaks.

5 Pronunciation linking

a 🔊 **1.33** Listen to six sentences. How many words do you hear? Circle the correct number. Contracted forms (e.g. *doesn't*) count as one word.

a 4 / 5 / 6
b 4 / 5 / 6
c 4 / 5 / 6
d 4 / 5 / 6
e 4 / 5 / 6
f 4 / 5 / 6

b 🔊 **1.33** Listen to the sentences again. Write the links between the consonants and the vowel sounds.

a John often travels abroad.
b Shannon and Nicole are always busy.
c He doesn't often have time.
d How often does Shannon surf?
e I read a newspaper every morning.
f Michael is often tired.

c 🔊 **1.33** Listen again and repeat the sentences.

4c Extreme sports

Vocabulary sports

1 Match these sports (1–8) with the equipment (a–h).

1. basketball
2. boxing
3. cricket
4. hockey
5. rowing
6. skiing
7. surfing
8. tennis

a

b

c

d

e

f

g

h

Listening an extreme sport

3 🔊 **1.34** Listen to an interview with Claude Geraldo, a base jumper. Tick the topics Claude talks about.

1. different types of extreme sports
2. a definition of base jumping
3. why he likes base jumping
4. base jumping with friends
5. how you learn to base jump
6. why base jumping is dangerous
7. base jumping competitions

4 🔊 **1.34** Listen again. Are the sentences true (T) or false (F)?

1. In base jumping, you parachute from an aeroplane.
2. Claude likes different sports.
3. You don't need to learn to parachute.
4. Claude isn't scared when he jumps.
5. He likes the adrenaline.
6. He thinks anyone can do this sport.
7. Base jumping is more dangerous than jumping from an aeroplane.
8. He thinks base jumping is the most dangerous extreme sport.

Grammar can/can't

5 Choose the correct option to complete the sentences.

1. *Can you / Can you to* play cricket?
2. I can play football well but I *can / can't* play basketball very well.
3. We can't ski *very well / not very well*.
4. Claude can speak *well English / English well*.
5. He *can / cans* run a marathon in three hours.
6. Sara *can't / don't can* hit the ball in tennis.
7. Can you play golf *well / not very well*?
8. *How well can you / How well do you can* surf?

2 Vocabulary extra sports equipment

Match the name of the sports equipment (1–8) with the pictures (a–h) from Exercise 1.

1. oars — *h*
2. racquet
3. bat
4. gloves
5. basket
6. skis
7. board
8. stick

32

4d A summer job

Listening interview for a summer job

1 🔊 **1.35** Hailey Gould has an interview for a job in the summer. Listen to the interview and complete the interviewer's form.

Job:	Children's summer school helper
Name:	Hailey Gould
Age:	1 _____
Nationality:	2 _____
Languages:	3 _____
Sports:	4 _____
Other skills:	5 _____

Real life talking about abilities and interests

2 Complete the extract from the interview (1–8) with these phrases (a–h).

a I can't start
b are you good at
c I can play tennis a bit
d how well can you speak
e I'm not very good at
f I can a bit
g can you speak
h do you like art

I = Interviewer, H = Hailey

I: So, ¹_____ Italian?
H: Yes, I was born there so I'm fluent.
I: On the summer school we teach French to the children. ²_____ French?
H: Yes, ³_____. It's elementary.
I: That's OK. We teach the children simple words and songs in French.
H: That's fine. I can do that.
I: We also do sports with the children. ⁴_____ playing tennis or football?
H: ⁵_____, and I'm not bad at basketball.
I: Good. And we also have activities with art and music. ⁶_____ or can you play a musical instrument?
H: ⁷_____ painting or art but I like playing the guitar.
I: That sounds great. When can you start? We need someone from the twentieth.
H: Oh sorry, ⁸_____ before the twenty-seventh.
I: Well, that might be OK …

3 🔊 **1.35** Listen again and check your answers.

4 Pronunciation sentence stress

🔊 **1.36** Listen to these sentences from the interview. Tick the sentence stress you hear.

1 a Can you <u>speak</u> <u>Italian</u>?
   b <u>Can</u> <u>you</u> speak Italian?
2 a <u>I</u> can <u>a</u> bit.
   b I <u>can</u> a <u>bit</u>.
3 a Are you <u>good</u> at <u>playing</u> <u>tennis</u>?
   b <u>Are</u> <u>you</u> good <u>at</u> playing tennis?
4 a Do you <u>like</u> <u>art</u>?
   b <u>Do</u> <u>you</u> like art?
5 a <u>I'm</u> not <u>very</u> good <u>at</u> painting.
   b I'm <u>not</u> very <u>good</u> at <u>painting</u>.

5 Grammar extra preposition + -ing

> **GRAMMAR preposition + -ing**
>
> When you use a verb after a preposition, use the -*ing* form of the verb. For example:
> Are you good **at** play**ing** tennis?
> I'm not very good **at** paint**ing**.

Complete the sentences with the -*ing* form of these verbs.

do	go	paint	play	~~speak~~	watch

1 I'm good at _____*speaking*_____ English.
2 I'm not very good at _____ my homework on time.
3 I'm bad at _____ football.
4 My brother is very good at _____ pictures of people.
5 Are you interested in _____ to the cinema?
6 Sorry, but I'm not interested in _____ this film.

6 Write true sentences for you. Use the -*ing* form.

1 I'm good at _____
2 I'm not very good at _____
3 I'm interested in _____
4 I'm not interested in _____

Unit 4 Free time

33

4e You have an email

Reading plans to meet

1 Number these emails in the correct order (1–8).

A
I'm at work until 2.30. But I work in the centre so I can meet you. Maybe we can have a late lunch afterwards?

B
Where is it? I don't know where you work.

C
Hello Sandy
Sorry, but when is it exactly? I'm in the office some of the time this weekend.

D
Hi again
Why are you there at the weekend?! Anyway, I think they come through between two and three on Saturday afternoon.

E
That sounds great! Can my cousin come to lunch too? She's with me until next week.

F
28 King Street

G
Hi Alex
Do you like watching cycling? There's a cycling race this weekend and the cyclists come through the centre of the city.

H
Sure, no problem. See you and her at 2.30. Meet me outside my office building.

2 Writing skill reference words

Read these sentences from the emails. Who or what does the underlined word refer to?

1 Why are you <u>there</u> at the weekend?
   at work
2 When is <u>it</u> exactly? _____
3 <u>She</u>'s with me until next week. _____
4 See <u>you</u> and her at 2.30. _____
5 Where is <u>it</u>? _____
6 I think <u>they</u> come through between two and three on Saturday afternoon. _____

3 Match sentences (1–6) with sentences (a–f) to make pairs.

1 My favourite café is The Coffee Stop.
2 We can meet but I can't leave the house today.
3 I have some money for Joe.
4 What's wrong with this computer?
5 I have two pens.
6 Why are Mike and Saleh here?

a It's very slow today.
b But one of them doesn't work.
c Can we meet there?
d Please tell him.
e Can you come here?
f I don't like them!

Writing short emails

4 You are at your desk at work. You receive this email from a colleague in another part of the building. Write a reply.

Hi!
Can you help me? My printer doesn't work. Are you good at fixing them?
And one other thing – it's the receptionist's birthday this evening. We have a table at Restaurant Italia after work at 6 p.m. Are you interested in coming too?
Matt

Wordbuilding verb + noun collocations

1 Match a verb with a noun and use them to complete these sentences.

do	go	listen to	meet	play	read
spend	watch				

article	chess	clients	a DVD	shopping
radio	time	work		

1 I never _____ at the weekend because the city centre is very crowded.
2 A lot of people don't _____ because they think it's a boring game. But I think it's relaxing.
3 I want to _____ the _____ because the news is on at midday.
4 I sometimes _____ in the evenings when we're very busy in the office.
5 _____ the _____ in this magazine. It's very interesting.
6 I often _____ in a nice café when we want to discuss contracts.
7 How much _____ do you _____ studying English a week?
8 I often _____ with my children. It's more fun than a computer game.

Learning skills learn vocabulary by reading

2 Reading is a great way to learn new vocabulary. Find interesting articles in English and write down new words and collocations.

Read this article about free time at work. There are a lot of collocations in the text (e.g. *go to work*). Underline the collocations and write them in your vocabulary notebook.

Check!

3 Read the clues and complete the words. The answers are in Unit 4 of the Student's Book.

1 What W is a US State with Snoqualmie Falls? W *ashington*
2 What T describes the people with the surname Mulgray, Kitt and Bryan? t_____
3 What H is a musical instrument? h_____
4 What PB does Norbert Rosing photograph? p_____ b_____
5 What G is Norbert from? G_____
6 What A does Norbert like going to? The A_____
7 What H is a sport where you put a line between two high places and walk across? h_____
8 What G is a type of year that students take? g_____

Free time at work

A lot of people go to work for eight hours a day and they spend all day on their computers. But information from a survey shows that office workers use their computers for other activities. In fact they spend an hour a day doing this.

1	They visit social networking sites	15 minutes a day
2	They play online games	10 minutes a day
3	They send emails to friends	10 minutes a day
4	They watch videos	10 minutes a day
5	They do online shopping	5 minutes a day
6	They search the Internet	10 minutes a day

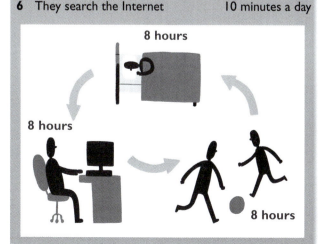

Unit 5 Food

5a Food journeys

Vocabulary food and food verbs

1 Choose the correct option (a or b) to complete these sentences.

1 We .... all the food in this restaurant by hand.
   a make   b taste
2 I like .... eggs for breakfast.
   a smelling   b eating
3 The waiters .... customers very quickly.
   a make   b serve
4 Do you .... the meat on the fire?
   a cook   b eat
5 Your soup .... delicious! Can I taste it?
   a serves   b smells

2 Complete the diagram with these food words.

| chicken | eggs | lamb | lemons | milk |
| onions | peppers | raisins | rice | salt |

3 Pronunciation number of syllables

1.37 Listen to the food words. How many syllables do you hear?

1 eggs — *1*   8 raisin
2 chicken — *2*   9 cheese
3 potato — *3*   10 pepper
4 lamb   11 fruit
5 lemon   12 dairy
6 oranges   13 seasoning
7 salt   14 onion

Reading discover food in the USA

4 Complete the article (1–5) with these sentences (a–e).

a This way they are very fresh and taste delicious.
b You can catch your own or there are a lot of great seafood restaurants on the coast.
c There's a festival in June and they serve a local dish called a peach cobbler.
d July is a good month to go because of the Vermont Cheesemaker's Festival.
e You walk through the town and taste chocolate at twenty different places.

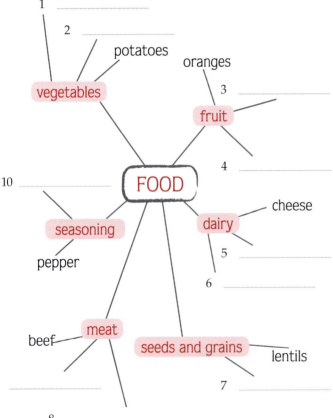

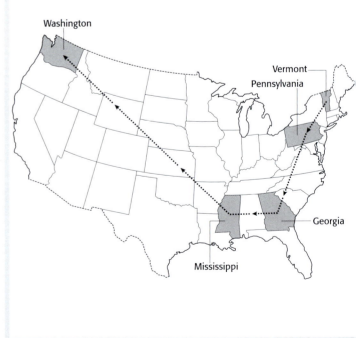

36

Food journey in the USA

You can find every type of food in the USA and every state has its favourite dish. Here are my top five.

1 **Cheese in Vermont**
   Vermont is famous for its cheese. Vermont Cheddar is the most famous, but you can taste different types of cheese at every time of year. [1] ....

2 **Pumpkins and chocolate in Pennsylvania**
   Drive from the state capital of Philadelphia into the countryside. In October, you can see beautiful orange pumpkins everywhere and a lot of towns have pumpkin festivals. And the town of Lititz also has a 'chocolate walk'. [2] ....

3 **Peaches in Georgia**
   Go south to the state of Georgia. The symbol of the state is a peach and June is the best month for peaches. [3] ....

4 **Shrimps in Mississippi**
   After Georgia, drive to the Mississippi Gulf Coast. Arrive early in the morning and meet the shrimp boats. You can buy white shrimps or brown shrimps. [4] ....

5 **Crab in Washington**
   For more seafood, drive northwest to the state of Washington. July is a good month for crabs. [5] ....

5 Read the article again. Answer these questions with *Yes*, *No* or *Don't know* (because the information isn't in the article).

1 Is there a good month for cheese in Vermont?
2 Is there a good month for pumpkins in Pennsylvania?
3 Who makes the chocolate in Lititz?
4 Is an apple the symbol of Georgia?
5 Is June a good month for peaches in Georgia?
6 Are the shrimps in Mississippi cheap?
7 Is there a good month for crabs in Washington?
8 Are there good restaurants in Washington next to the sea?

Grammar countable and uncountable nouns (*a*, *some* and *any*)

6 Are these nouns countable or uncountable? Write C or U.

1 onion — C
2 bread — U
3 juice
4 carrot
5 pasta
6 banana
7 lemon
8 pumpkin
9 cheese
10 peach

7 Complete the sentences with these words.

| a | an | any | some |

1 I'd like .... salt, please.
2 We need .... onion.
3 There's .... lemon in the fridge.
4 Do you need .... cheese?
5 We don't have .... milk.
6 This is .... peach from Georgia.
7 I'd like .... orange, please.
8 We need .... bread for breakfast.

5b People and food

Grammar *a lot of* and *not much / not many*

1 Complete the questionnaire with *a lot of*, *much* or *many*. In some sentences, two options are possible. Then tick the sentences which are healthy.

How healthy are you?

1 I eat _a lot of_ fruit and vegetables.
2 I eat _____ meat, cheese and bread.
3 I don't eat _____ desserts.
4 I don't eat _____ salad.
5 I do _____ sports.
6 I don't do _____ free-time activities like dancing or gardening.
7 I drink _____ water.
8 I don't buy _____ fresh food.

2 Listen and respond questions about food and health

🔊 **1.38** A health expert uses the questionnaire in Exercise 1 to ask questions. Listen to the questions and answer for you. Use these answers.

Yes, I do.   No, not much.   No, not many.

Vocabulary quantities and containers

3 Which food or drink does not come in these quantities or containers? Delete it from the list.

1 A BAG OF   ~~water~~, pasta, rice
2 A BOTTLE OF   milk, water, bread
3 A CUP OF   tea, coffee, chicken
4 A KILO OF   rice, potatoes, juice
5 A GLASS OF   milk, apple juice, eggs
6 A PIECE OF   chocolate, coffee, cake
7 A SLICE OF   bread, salt, pizza
8 A TIN OF   fish, soup, chocolate

4 Complete the sentences with a quantity or container word from Exercise 3.

1 Can you open the _____ of rice, please?
2 Would like a _____ of water or just a glass?
3 That chocolate looks delicious. Could I have a small _____ ?
4 Open the _____ of soup and pour it into the bowl.
5 I always have a _____ of coffee in the morning with breakfast.
6 A: There's a lot of pasta in this packet.
    B: Yes, it's a _____ .
7 I'm really hungry. Can I have two _____ of pizza, please?
8 A: Would you like some water?
    B: Yes, please. I'd like a _____ of sparkling water.
    A: Large or small?

Listening talking about food

5 🔊 **1.39** Listen to six conversations. Match the conversations (1–6) with the situations (a–f).

Conversation 1 ....
Conversation 2 ....
Conversation 3 ....
Conversation 4 ....
Conversation 5 ....
Conversation 6 ....

a Two friends plan a picnic.
b A customer wants to make curry.
c A friend has something from Switzerland.
d A waiter and customer in a restaurant.
e A customer wants something for a barbecue.
f Two friends at breakfast.

6 🔊 **1.39** Listen again. Answer the questions for each conversation.

Conversation 1
1 Does the customer want sparkling or still water?

2 Does the customer want a glass or a bottle?

Conversation 2
3 How much rice does the customer want?

Conversation 3
4 Is the sauce hot?

5 Is the sauce in a bottle or a tin?

Conversation 4
6 What does the person offer?

Conversation 5
7 How much bread does the person want?

Conversation 6
8 What is the tuna in?

Grammar *how many / how much*

7 Make eight questions with the words in the table.

How	many / much	rice	do you want?
		apples	
		bread	
		eggs	
		pasta	
		packets of pasta	
		chocolate	
		bananas	

1 *How much rice do you want?*
2 ....
3 ....
4 ....
5 ....
6 ....
7 ....
8 ....

8 Match these responses (a–h) with the questions (1–8) from Exercise 7.

a Three red ones and three green, please.
b I'd like a box of six, please.
c A small piece.
d Not much. I don't like Italian food.
e Two slices, please. And some butter.
f Two, please. I have a lot of people for dinner so I need it for making spaghetti Bolognese.
g A kilo of brown and a kilo of white. It's for an Indian dish.
h I need six but those are brown. Do you have any yellow ones?

Unit 5 Food

39

5c Space food

Listening food for astronauts

1 🔊 **1.40** Listen to three parts of a documentary about space. Number these topics in the order you hear them (1–3).

a the problems of food in space
b space food in the future
c how you eat and drink in space

Glossary
float (v) /fləʊt/ fly in the air because there is no gravity
gravity (n) /ˈɡrævəti/ force that pulls objects down to the Earth

2 🔊 **1.40** Listen to the three parts again. Choose the correct ending (a–c) to complete these sentences.

1 Space food is difficult to _____.
  a transport into space
  b cook in space
  c buy in space
2 In space, food and drink _____.
  a don't move
  b fall to the ground
  c fly through the air
3 The menu on a modern space ship is _____.
  a different from food on Earth
  b the same as food on Earth
  c bad
4 Astronauts _____.
  a can choose their food
  b can't choose their food
  c don't eat food
5 In space, astronauts _____.
  a eat at night
  b eat one big meal a day
  c eat three meals a day
6 On the International Space Station, they recycle water from the air _____.
  a outside the space station
  b inside the space station
  c on Earth
7 In the future, scientists plan to grow food in space so humans can live there for _____.
  a days
  b months
  c years

Word focus *of*

3 🔊 **1.41** Match the sentence beginnings (1–5) with the endings (a–e). Then listen and check your answers.

1 A lot of
2 The People's Republic of
3 I'd like a cup of
4 I'm always tired in the middle of
5 There are many different types of

a China is famous for its Great Wall.
b people like chicken.
c fruit and vegetables in this market.
d tea, please.
e the afternoon.

4 **Pronunciation** linking *of*

🔊 **1.41** Listen again and repeat the sentences in Exercise 3. Remember to link *of*.

A lot of people like chicken.

5d At the restaurant

Vocabulary a menu

1 Complete the menu with these words.

| desserts | drinks | main course | salads |
| soups | starters | | |

Tommy's Taverna

1 ....
Garlic bread   £4.45
Prawn salad   £4.95

2 ....
Tomato   £2.95
Onion   £2.95

3 ....
Chicken kabsa   £9.50
Lamb moussaka   £10.95
All dishes come with a choice of vegetables.

4 ....
             Small   Large
Green   £3.50   £6.00
Caesar   £3.95   £7.95

5 ....
Cheesecake   £5.25
Ice cream   £4.50

6 ....
Bottle of water (sparkling or still)   £1.50
Tea or coffee   £1.25

Real life ordering a meal

2 ▶ 1.42 Listen to three parts of a conversation in the restaurant. Notice the waiter's mistake (bottle, not glass). Circle five more mistakes.

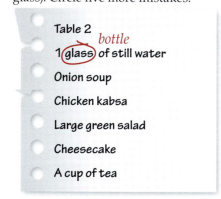

Table 2
1 ~~glass~~ bottle of still water
Onion soup
Chicken kabsa
Large green salad
Cheesecake
A cup of tea

3 Put these words in order to make phrases. Then complete the conversation with the phrases.

a can I anything you get
   ....

b menu is here the
   ....

c water I'd some like
   ....

d green salad I'll a small have
   ....

e have I bill could the
   ....

f a cup I'd coffee like of
   ....

g delicious that was
   ....

h ready to you order are
   ....

W = Waiter, C = Customer
W: Here's your table. And ¹................ . ²................ to drink first?
C: Yes, ³................ , please.
W: Sparkling or still?
C: Still, please. Actually, I'll have sparkling. A bottle.
W: OK.

W: Here you are. And ⁴................ ?
C: Yes, I'll have tomato soup and then the chicken kabsa sounds interesting.
W: Yes, it's a Middle Eastern dish.
C: Great.
W: And would you like a small salad with that?
C: Err, yes. ⁵................ .

W: Finished?
C: Yes, thanks. ⁶................ .
W: Any dessert?
C: Err, no, I don't want a dessert, but ⁷................ .
W: Sure.
C: And ⁸................ , please?

4 ▶ 1.42 Listen again and check your answers.

5 Pronunciation contracted forms

▶ 1.43 Listen and tick the sentence you hear.
1 a I'd like a bottle of water.
   b I would like a bottle of water.
2 a We'd like dessert.
   b We would like dessert.
3 a They'd like a pizza.
   b They would like a pizza.
4 a He'd like soup.
   b He would like soup.

5e Instructions

1 Vocabulary extra cooking verbs

Complete the cooking instructions with these verbs.

chop   slice   mix   pour   put   spread

1 _____ the chicken with the rice.
2 _____ the onion into small pieces.
3 _____ the hot water onto the vegetables.
4 _____ the chicken in the oven.
5 _____ the butter on the bread with a knife.
6 _____ the bread with a knife.

2 Dictation cooking instructions

🎧 1.44 Listen to some instructions for making pasta with a pasta machine. Write the missing words.

a pasta machine

You can buy pasta in a ¹ _____
pasta and it tastes better. ² _____
flour and olive oil. ³ _____
_____ in a bowl and
⁴ _____.
Knead the mixture and make a ball of dough.
⁵ _____
⁶ _____
dough through the machine until it is very flat. Then ⁷ _____
_____ thin strips with a knife.

3 Writing skill punctuation

Read and check your punctuation in Exercise 2. Compare your punctuation with the audioscript on page 119.

Writing instructions

4 The pictures are instructions for scrambled eggs. Use these words to write the instruction for each picture.

put   eggs   bowl   pour   milk
mix   cook   frying pan   plate

1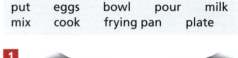

2

3

4

5

Scrambled eggs
1 _____
2 _____
3 _____
4 _____
5 _____

Unit 5 Food

Wordbuilding British or American English?

1 Label the pictures with these words in British English.

pavement	motorway	lift	full stop
mobile phone	petrol	chips	bill
football	biscuit		

1 ....

2 ....

3 ....

4 ....

5 ....

6 ....

7 ....

8 ....

9 ....

10 ....

2 Match the American English words (a–j) with the British English words (1–10) in Exercise 1.
 a freeway
 b elevator
 c cell phone
 d fries
 e period
 f check
 g sidewalk
 h soccer
 i gas
 j cookie

3 Replace one word in each sentence to change it from British English to American English.
 1 Can you put some ~~petrol~~ in the car? *gas*
 2 Take the lift to the top of the building.
 3 Can I use your mobile phone, please?
 4 Do you want a biscuit with your tea?
 5 Do you like playing football?
 6 The speed limit on the motorway is 70 miles per hour.
 7 My food was delicious! Can I have the bill now?
 8 Always use a full stop at the end of a sentence.

Learning skills dictionary skills (1)

4 It's a good idea to look up new words in an English learner dictionary. But do you know how to use a dictionary? Match the different parts of the dictionary (1–8) with the information (a–h).

> 1 **bread** /bred/ noun [U] food made from flour, water and yeast
>
> **chip** /tʃɪp/ noun [C] 1 a piece of potato cooked in hot oil (AmE. fry) 2 a small piece of silicon with electronic connections used in computers
>
> **kitchen** /ˈkɪtʃən/ noun [C] a room where people cook food

 a the spelling of the word
 b the definition of the word
 c the type of word (noun, verb, adjective)
 d the noun is countable
 e the pronunciation of the word
 f the word in American English
 g the noun is uncountable
 h the word's second meaning

Check!

5 How much can you remember about these international dishes? Complete the table with notes. Then check your answers in Unit 5 of the Student's Book.

The dish	Which country is famous for this dish?	Which food is usually in it?
kabsa	*Saudi Arabia*	
pizza		
ceviche		
pierogi		

43

Unit 6 Money

6a Money on the move

1 Vocabulary extra verbs + money

Complete these extracts from five texts with the correct verb.

1 You can e_____ over £20 an hour by working from home. The hours are flexible and the work is rewarding. Call 0207 867 777 today!

2 We need your help today. Please g_____ money and help the animals.

3 We offer great rates on euros, dollars and other currencies. There is no interest when you c_____ over £300.

4 When you s_____ over $50, we give you $5 off your next purchase.

5 S_____ your money with us and your money is safe!

2 Where are the texts in Exercise 1 from? Match them with these places (a–e).

a a bank
b a currency exchange
c an advert for a job
d a shop
e a charity poster

Reading money on the move

3 Read the article. Match the headings (a–c) with the paragraphs (1–3).

a Advice on money from blogging
b How Torre's blog became popular
c Who makes money from blogging?

4 Complete the article (1–5) with these sentences (a–e).

a Successful bloggers can also sell advertising and sell travel products.
b about something you love doing.
c And Hollywood is interested in making a film of the book.
d There were lots of stories on the blog for her family to read.
e For example, twenty-year-olds in South America who like adventure sports.

Money on the move

1 _____
Torre DeRoche writes a travel blog called *The Fearful Adventurer*. At first, it was a blog for her family because she was on a boat in the middle of the Pacific Ocean. ¹ *d* But after a few months the blog was popular with lots of other people on the Internet. Now Torre has a new book about her life of travel. ² _____

2 _____
Other people also make money from writing on the Internet. The travel writer Gary Arndt writes on his blog about travelling round the world and earns money from writing online. ³ _____ But not everyone is successful. Gary says there are lots of travel blogs, but only a small number of people earn a living from them.

3 _____
But if you love travel and you love writing, then a blog is fun. And if you want to earn some money then write:
• about something new and interesting.
• for one type of reader. ⁴ _____
• on social networking sites like Facebook or Twitter so people can find your blog.
• ⁵ _____

Grammar was/were

5 Read more about the writer Torre DeRoche. Choose the correct verb.

Torre DeRoche ¹(was) / were born in Australia, but her parents ² was / were from California. Her mother ³ was / were a singer and her father ⁴ was / were a writer.

In her mid twenties, Torre DeRoche ⁵ was / were a graphic designer in San Francisco with her boyfriend. But they ⁶ were / weren't interested in money and a career so, a year later, they left the USA, on a boat. They ⁷ was / were on the Pacific Ocean for two years. Sometimes life ⁸ wasn't / weren't easy on the boat but Torre wrote about her adventures on a travel blog. Soon the blog ⁹ was / were popular with readers all around the world.

6 Make questions about Torre DeRoche for these answers. Use *was* and *were*.

1 Where _____?
  California.
2 What _____?
  A writer.
3 _____ in money?
  No, she wasn't.
4 How long _____?
  For two years.
5 Who _____ with?
  Readers all around the world.

7 Pronunciation was/were

🔊 **1.45** Listen to *was*, *were*, *wasn't* and *weren't* in these sentences. When do we stress the verb: in affirmative sentences, negative sentences and/or questions?

1 George Washington was the President.
2 He wasn't on the dollar.
3 Was he the President?
4 Kahlo and Rivera were artists.
5 They weren't Spanish.
6 Were they artists?

Vocabulary age

8 Replace the words in bold in the sentences with words from the table.

in	my your his her our their	early mid late	twenties thirties forties fifties sixties

1 I was a student **when I was 22**.
  I was a student *in my early twenties*.
2 You were married **when you were 35**.
  You were married _____.
3 She was a manager **when she was 48**.
  She was a manager _____.
4 We were grandparents **when we were 62**.
  We were grandparents _____.
5 He was a millionaire **when he was 59**.
  He was a millionaire _____.
6 They weren't interested in money **when they were 25**.
  They weren't interested in money _____.

6b Finding money

Listening talking about money

1 🔊 **1.46** Listen to four people talking about money. Answer the questions.

1 Person 1: Did this person win a TV or win money from a TV show?

2 Person 2: Did this person work long hours and earn extra money?

3 Person 3: What is the TV programme about?

4 Person 4: Who has a new business: the speaker or his friend?

2 🔊 **1.46** Listen again. How does each person feel? Match the people (1–4) with the adjectives (a–d).

Person 1   a bored
Person 2   b excited
Person 3   c interested
Person 4   d tired

Vocabulary -ed/-ing adjectives

3 Complete the adjectives in these pairs of sentences with -ed or -ing.

1 a This book is very interest_____.
    b I'm very interest_____ in old objects.
2 a Ingmar is very excit_____ about his new job.
    b Earning money for the first time is excit_____.
3 a Doing the same job for many years can be very bor_____.
    b At school I was bor_____ in History but now I like it.

4 Complete these sentences for you with the name of a free-time activity.

1 I'm interested in _____.
2 _____ is boring.
3 _____ is an exciting hobby.

Grammar past simple (affirmative): regular and irregular verbs

▶ **SPELL CHECK verbs + -ed**
- Add -ed to verbs ending in a consonant: want → wanted
- Add -d to verbs ending in -e: arrive → arrived
- Double the final consonant in some verbs ending with a vowel and a consonant: stop → stopped
- For some verbs ending with -y, change the -y to -i: study → studied

5 Write the past simple form of these verbs.

1 live _____
2 work _____
3 discover _____
4 phone _____
5 study _____
6 pay _____
7 receive _____
8 die _____

6 pronunciation -ed endings

🔊 **1.47** The -ed endings of regular verbs can have three different sounds: /t/, /d/ or /ɪd/. Listen and circle the ending you hear.

1 liked   **(/t/)**   /d/   /ɪd/
2 lived   /t/   **(/d/)**   /ɪd/
3 decided   /t/   /d/   **(/ɪd/)**
4 wanted   /t/   /d/   /ɪd/
5 worked   /t/   /d/   /ɪd/
6 started   /t/   /d/   /ɪd/
7 played   /t/   /d/   /ɪd/
8 visited   /t/   /d/   /ɪd/
9 travelled   /t/   /d/   /ɪd/
10 arrived   /t/   /d/   /ɪd/
11 danced   /t/   /d/   /ɪd/
12 showed   /t/   /d/   /ɪd/

7 Dictation my past life

🔊 **1.48** Someone is talking about their past life. Listen and write their words.

8 Complete the text with the past simple form of these regular and irregular verbs.

Lost ship discovered

In 1533, a Portuguese ship ¹_____ (go) from Portugal to India. It ²_____ (have) gold and diamonds to buy spices in India. But at the southern part of Africa, the weather ³_____ (be) bad and the ship never ⁴_____ (arrive). It sank and the crew ⁵_____ (die).

Five hundred years later, a geologist in Namibia ⁶_____ (discover) a small piece of metal in the Orange River. It was money. Later, archaeologists ⁷_____ (pull) more coins from the river. But there were also parts of a ship – the Portuguese ship. For the archaeologists these were more important than the gold because they ⁸_____ (give) information about people's lives five hundred years ago.

Glossary
sank (past tense of *sink*) /sæŋk/ go down under the sea

6c Mobile cash

Listening M-Pesa

1 🔘 **1.49** Listen to part of a radio documentary. What is it about? Choose the correct answer (a–d).

   a   a modern way to go shopping in Kenya
   b   a modern and popular way to pay money in Kenya
   c   why people don't use banks in Kenya
   d   why it's difficult to use money in Kenya

2 🔘 **1.49** Listen again. Choose the correct answer (a–c) for these questions.

   1   How does the man pay for his petrol at the garage?
       a   with cash
       b   with a credit card
       c   with his mobile phone
   2   How long does he wait to pay?
       a   not long
       b   a long time
       c   an hour
   3   When did M-Pesa begin in Kenya?
       a   2007
       b   2010
       c   2012
   4   Where can you use M-Pesa?
       a   only in the cities
       b   only in the countryside
       c   in a lot of places
   5   Where can you put money on your phone?
       a   in a bank
       b   in a shop
       c   in a foreign exchange
   6   Who sends the text?
       a   the person who buys
       b   the person who sells
       c   the person in the M-Pesa shop
   7   Who gives the cash?
       a   the person who buys
       b   the person who sells
       c   the person in the shop
   8   What is M-Pesa an example of?
       a   how mobile technology changes our lives
       b   how money changes our lives
       c   how shopping changes our lives

3 **Vocabulary extra** ways of payment

   Match these ways of payment with the definitions (1–6).

bank transfer	cheque	coins
credit card	debit card	notes

   1   ....: paper money
   2   ....: metal cash
   3   ....: You write the name of a person or a company and the amount on it.
   4   ....: You pay with this piece of plastic and the money comes immediately from your bank account.
   5   ....: You pay with this piece of plastic, but you don't pay the money immediately.
   6   ....: You move money from your bank account to another bank account.

6d Help!

1 Vocabulary extra opposite words

Complete the pairs of sentences with these words.

1 buy / sell
   a I'd like to _____ a kilo of flour, please.
   b What does this shop _____?

2 give / take
   a Can you _____ some money to this charity?
   b Don't _____ all my coins. I need them for the coffee machine.

3 save / spend
   a Don't _____ all your money in the shops!
   b How much money do you _____ in your bank account every month?

4 lend / borrow
   a Can you _____ me five euros?
   b You can _____ five euros from me.

Real life requesting

2 🎵 **1.50** Listen to four requests. Does the other person respond with *Yes* or *No*?

Request 1 _____
Request 2 _____
Request 3 _____
Request 4 _____

3 🎵 **1.50** Complete the four conversations (1–8) with these requests and responses (a–h). Then listen again and check.

a Can I ask you something?
b Could you lend me some?
c Can I borrow some money?
d Could you give us some money today?
e I'm afraid I don't have any money.
f Yes, certainly.
g I'm sorry, but I can't.
h Yes, of course.

1 A: Hello. I'm with a local charity. We collect money for a local hospital. We want to buy some new medical equipment for the children's part of the hospital.
   ¹_____
   B: Err, ²_____
   A: Oh dear. Well, there's a bank around the corner so you could get some money.

2 A: Hello, ³_____
   B: ⁴_____ What's the problem?
   A: Well, I want to transfer money online from one bank account to another. But I can't open my account.
   B: You need a password.
   A: Oh! Do I?

3 A: Sorry, but I don't have any money until the end of the month. ⁵_____
   B: How much?
   A: Two hundred?
   B: Two hundred! ⁶_____
   A: Well, what about one hundred?

4 A: Hi. ⁷_____
   B: How much?
   A: Just a pound. I want a cup of coffee from the machine.
   B: ⁸_____ Here you are.

4 Pronunciation polite intonation

a 🎵 **1.51** Listen to the requests. Does the intonation sound friendly and polite, or unfriendly and impolite?

1 Can you help me?   ☺ ☹
2 Could you lend me some money?   ☺ ☹
3 Can I borrow some money?   ☺ ☹
4 Could you give me some help?   ☺ ☹

b 🎵 **1.52** Listen and repeat the four requests from Part a with friendly and polite intonation.

5 Listen and respond responding to requests

🎵 **1.53** Listen to four requests. Respond with a polite response. Then compare your response with the model answer that follows.

1 Respond *Yes*
2 Respond *No*
3 Respond *No*
4 Respond *Yes*

6e Thank you messages

1 Writing skill formal and informal expressions

Complete the thank you messages with these words and phrases.

> Best regards   Dear Mrs   Hi
> I look forward to   Love   See you
> Thank you for   Thank you very much
> Thanks   Yours sincerely

---

1 _____ Auntie Gina
2 _____ for the money!
It's useful for my new life as a university student!
See you in the holidays.
3 _____
Karen

Subject: Conference in Oslo
Dear Bram
4 _____ your work in Oslo. We were pleased with the conference and we enjoyed our evening out. Everyone in the team sends their thanks.
5 _____ again next year.
6 _____
Ivan

---

7 _____ Adamson
8 _____ for your interest in R.J. Fashions and our new range of clothing. Please find enclosed our catalogue for the new season.
9 _____ hearing from you in the future.
10 _____
R.J. Jones

Writing thank you messages

2 Write three different thank you messages. Read the situation and use the correct formal or informal expressions.

1 A friend lent you some money. Return the money as a cheque. Write a short thank you message.

2 You were in another country for work and spent two days with a work colleague. Write a thank you email.

3 You work for a holiday company. Someone wants information about your holidays. Write a letter and send a brochure.

Wordbuilding compound nouns

> **WORDBUILDING compound nouns**
>
> We make compound nouns with two nouns. For example:
> *house + work = housework*
> *credit + card = credit card*
>
> Sometimes the two words are together. For example:
> *bath + room = bathroom*
> *foot + ball = football*
>
> Sometimes the two words are separate. For example:
> *mobile + phone = mobile phone*
> *cash + machine = cash machine*

1 Make compound nouns from Units 1–6 with these words. Then complete the sentences.

| arm | basket | credit | full | mobile |
| roller | post | tourist | | |

| ball | blades | card | chair | office |
| information | phone | stop | | |

1. How often do you play _____?
2. Do you pay by _____ or with cash?
3. _____ helps visitors in a new city.
4. Please switch off your _____ in the library.
5. Sit down in this _____. It's very comfortable.
6. Always use a _____ at the end of a sentence.
7. My daughter likes her new _____. She can move very quickly on them.
8. Can you send these letters at the _____?

Learning skills consider your learning

2 You are in the middle of this course. Think about your learning using this questionnaire. Circle the number in Part 1 and answer the questions in Part 2. Then show the questionnaire to your teacher and discuss your answers.

Your learning

4 = Very good   3 = Good
2 = Satisfactory   1 = Not very good

1 How was your progress in …?

Vocabulary	4	3	2	1
Grammar	4	3	2	1
Useful phrases (in 'Real life')	4	3	2	1
Pronunciation	4	3	2	1
Reading	4	3	2	1
Listening	4	3	2	1
Speaking	4	3	2	1
Writing	4	3	2	1

2 To help your learning …

What do you want more of in class?

....

What can you do at home?

....

Check!

3 There are a lot of people in Unit 6 of the Student's Book. Can you remember who they are, where they are from and why they are famous? Complete this table. Then check your answers in Unit 6 of the Student's Book.

	Person	Country	Reason for fame
1	George Washington	USA	
2			artists
3		Switzerland	
4			writer
5		England	archaeologist

Unit 7 Journeys

7a Famous journeys

Vocabulary travel verbs

1 Complete the sentences with these verbs.

| cycle | drive | fly | sail | take | travel |

1 One day I'd like to be a pilot and _____ around the world.
2 I can't _____ a car because I'm only fifteen.
3 I have a new bicycle so I can _____ to work every day.
4 I always _____ public transport because the roads in the city centre are very busy.
5 Is it difficult to _____ a ship?
6 Do you _____ by train or by bus?

2 Vocabulary extra land, sea and air

a Write these words in the correct groups. Use a dictionary to help you.

aeroplane	bicycle	boat	car	drive
fly	hot air balloon	sail	ship	train
walk	wheels	wings		

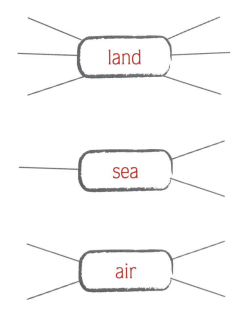

b Can you add more words to the three groups?

Grammar past simple: negatives

3 Complete the three texts with the past simple negative form of the verbs.

A The Spirit of St Louis
The Orteig Prize was $25,000. Raymond Orteig was a rich businessman and he offered the prize in 1919 to the first pilot to fly non-stop from New York to Paris. It was a dangerous journey and before 1927 six pilots tried the journey but they [1] _____ (survive). But in 1927, Charles Lindbergh flew from New York to Paris. It took 33 hours. He [2] _____ (stop) and so he won the Orteig Prize. Lindbergh and his plane, *The Spirit of St Louis*, became famous. You can see the plane today at the National Air and Space Museum in Washington.

B The Victoria
On 10th August 1519, five ships left Seville in Spain: the *Trinidad*, the *San Antonio*, the *Concepción*, the *Santiago* and the *Victoria*. Ferdinand Magellan was the leader of the five ships. They travelled across the ocean and arrived in a port in Brazil. After Brazil, Magellan's journey is famous because he sailed round the southern tip of South America. But Magellan [3] _____ (return) to Spain. He died in the Philippines and only the *Victoria* finished the journey. There is a replica of the ship in Punta Arenas in Chile, at the beginning of the Straits of Magellan.

C Sputnik

Sputnik was the first satellite from Earth into space. Humans ⁴ _____ (travel) inside *Sputnik* but they sent the satellite into space on 4th January 1957. As the satellite started to orbit Earth, people looked for it in the sky. It travelled round Earth 1,440 times and ⁵ _____ (enter) Earth's atmosphere again until 4th January 1958. Nowadays, there are replicas of *Sputnik 1* in different museums. More importantly, there are thousands of satellites orbiting Earth because of *Sputnik 1*'s journey.

Reading three famous journeys

4 Read about the three journeys in Exercise 3 again. Answer the questions for each journey.

1 Where was each journey: on land, sea, air or somewhere else?

A _____
B _____
C _____

2 What transport did they use?

A _____
B _____
C _____

5 Match the sentences (1–8) with the texts (A–C).

1 Other people tried the same journey, but they didn't succeed.
2 He didn't stop on the journey.
3 He didn't return to his country.
4 He won some money because of the journey.
5 There were a group of them on the journey.
6 The journey took 33 hours.
7 You can see it in a museum and it isn't a replica.

Grammar past simple questions

6 Write questions for these answers about the three journeys.

1 What _____ in 1919?
A prize of $25,000 to the first pilot to fly non-stop from New York to Paris.

2 When _____ ?
In 1927.

3 How long _____ ?
33 hours.

4 When _____ Spain?
On 10th August 1519.

5 Where _____ ?
In the Philippines.

6 At night, what _____ in the sky?
Sputnik.

7 How many times _____ _____ ?
1,440 times.

8 When _____ Earth's atmosphere?
On 4th January 1958.

53

7b Land, sea and air

Vocabulary journey adjectives

1 Match the pairs of adjectives (1–4) with the four pictures (a–d).

1 short and easy ....
2 long and slow ....
3 fast and dangerous ....
4 difficult but safe ....

Listening animals on land, in the sea and in the air

2 🔊 2.1 Listen to a nature documentary about these three animals. Answer the questions with a number.

Albatross

1 How far does an albatross fly in its lifetime? .... kilometres
2 How long are the wings of an adult albatross? .... metres
3 How far can it fly to feed a chick? .... kilometres

Zebra

4 How many zebras are in the middle of Africa? ....
5 How far is their migration? .... kilometres

Elephant seal

6 How far can an elephant seal travel on a journey? .... kilometres
7 How far can it dive? .... metres

Glossary

chick (n) /tʃɪk/ a baby bird

3 🔊 **2.1** Listen again. Complete these sentences.
1 The wings of an albatross _____ on Earth.
2 These beautiful animals are famous for their black and white coats, but their lives _____ because of their long journey.
3 The ocean around Antarctica _____ but for the elephant seals it is their home.
4 They can stay under the water _____ and only come up for air for a few minutes.

Grammar comparative adjectives

4 Look at the sentences in Exercise 3. Underline examples of comparative adjectives.

> ▶ **SPELL CHECK comparative adjectives**
> - Add *-er* to short adjectives to form the comparative: *old* → *older*
> - Add *-r* to adjectives ending in *-e*: *large* → *larger*
> - Change adjectives ending in *-y* (after a consonant) to *-i*, and add *-er*: *happy* → *happier*
> - Double the final consonant on some adjectives ending with a vowel and a consonant: *hot* → *hotter*

5 Look at the spell check box. Write the comparative form of these adjectives.
1 short _____
2 easy _____
3 big _____
4 busy _____
5 cheap _____
6 sad _____
7 wet _____
8 nice _____

6 Complete these sentences with the comparative form of the adjective in brackets.
1 This laptop is _____ (cheap) than that one.
2 I love the summer because it's _____. (hot)
3 Everything is _____ (expensive) at the airport shops.
4 Your new car is _____ (fast) than your old one.
5 The city is _____ (safe) during the day. At night it can be dangerous.
6 Are you _____ (old) than me?
7 I can speak Japanese but my brother is _____. (good)
8 Why are your results from school _____ (bad) than last year?

Word focus *than*

7 Use the prompts to make comparative sentences.
1 my brother / short / me
   My brother is shorter than me.
2 walking / slow / cycling
3 I think / rock climbing / difficult / surfing
4 giraffes / tall / elephants
5 camping / cheap / staying in a hotel
6 Canada / big / Iceland
7 a taxi / expensive / a public bus
8 cities / crowded / towns

8 🔊 **2.2** Listen and check your answers.

9 Pronunciation stressed syllables

🔊 **2.2** Listen again and underline the stressed syllables in your sentences from Exercise 7.
My <u>bro</u>ther is <u>shor</u>ter than <u>me</u>.

7c Journey to the seamounts

Listening mountains under the sea

1 🔊 **2.3** Listen to a documentary about seamounts. Number these topics in the order you hear them (1–3).

a the location of Las Gemelas
b a description of seamounts
c the journey to Las Gemelas

2 🔊 **2.3** Listen again. Are the sentences true (T) or false (F)?

1 You can see seamounts above the sea.
2 About 100,000 seamounts are over a kilometre high.
3 The journey to a lot of seamounts is short and easy.
4 Las Gemelas is an area of seamounts about 500 kilometres from the coast of Canada.
5 There is sea life on the sides of Las Gemelas.
6 Three people went to Las Gemelas in DeepSee.
7 They can't see the bottom of the seamounts.
8 A lot of seamounts are from volcanoes.

Avi Klapfer, Gregory Stone and Brian Skerry in the submersible DeepSee

Grammar superlative adjectives

> ▶ **SPELL CHECK** superlative adjectives
> - Add *-est* to short adjectives to form the comparative: *old* → *oldest*
> - Add *-st* to adjectives ending in *-e*: *large* → *largest*
> - Change adjectives ending in *-y* (after a consonant) to *-i*, and add *-est*: *happy* → *happiest*
> - Double the final consonant on some adjectives ending with a vowel and a consonant: *hot* → *hottest*

3 Look at the spell check box. Write the superlative form of these adjectives.

1 short
2 easy
3 big
4 slow
5 cheap
6 fast
7 sad
8 nice

4 Complete the sentences with the superlative form of these adjectives.

| busy | easy | far | good | high | large |
| populated | short | | | | |

1 The .... part of the seamount Las Gemelas is 2,286 metres.
2 The .... view of seamounts is from a submersible.
3 There are five oceans and the Pacific Ocean is the ....
4 In the northern hemisphere of the Earth, the .... day of the year is on 21st December.
5 Shanghai is the .... city on Earth. There are eighteen million people.
6 Neptune is the .... planet from the Sun.
7 Some people think English is the .... language to learn, but I think it's difficult!
8 Atlanta airport is the .... airport in the world. Over 38 million passengers travel through the airport every year.

7d How was your trip?

Vocabulary *journey, travel* or *trip*?

1 Complete these sentences with *journey*, *travel* or *trip*.

1 It's a long _____ from Cape Town to Cairo.
2 I don't like to _____ .
3 My manager is away on a business _____ .
4 Lots of students _____ during their holidays.
5 We went on a _____ to Amsterdam last weekend.
6 My _____ along the Andes mountains took 30 days.

Real life asking about a trip

2 🔊 **2.4** Listen to five short conversations. Match the conversations (1–5) with the topics (a–e).

Conversation 1   a the journey
Conversation 2   b the weather
Conversation 3   c the food
Conversation 4   d the hotel
Conversation 5   e business meeting

3 🔊 **2.4** Listen again. Tick the response (a–c) you hear.

1 How was your flight?
 a Very good, thank you.
 b Very uncomfortable.
 c Tiring.
2 Was your hotel comfortable?
 a No, it wasn't and the Internet didn't work.
 b Yes, it was fine, but the Internet didn't work.
 c No, it wasn't, but the Internet worked.
3 How was your meeting?
 a Really useful.
 b Really interesting.
 c Very interesting.
4 What's the weather like?
 a Not bad.
 b Great!
 c Terrible.

5 Did you try the local food?
 a Yes, it's very hot and spicy.
 b Yes, it's delicious.
 c Yes, but I didn't enjoy it.

4 Pronunciation intonation in questions

🔊 **2.5** Listen to the questions and repeat with the correct intonation.
1 How was your journey?
2 How was your hotel?
3 Did you have dinner at the hotel?
4 What was the food like?
5 How was the meeting?
6 How was the weather?

5 Listen and respond questions about a trip

🔊 **2.6** Listen to the questions again and respond with an answer.

7e Writing about journeys

Vocabulary online writing

1 Complete the pairs of sentences with these words.

1. blog / website
   a I have my own _____. I write about my life and put pictures of my family on it.
   b I buy all my clothes from this _____.
2. blogger / writer
   a Charles Dickens was a famous English _____ in the nineteenth century.
   b Andrew Evans is a _____ on the *National Geographic* website.
3. homepage / online
   a I need to go _____. Is there Wi-Fi in the café?
   b Can you give me the address for the _____?
4. upload / download
   a I want to _____ photos of my holiday so all my family can see them online.
   b I can't _____ the photos of our holiday. Are you sure they are there?
5. post / comment
   a I read your latest blog and wrote a _____ afterwards. Did you see it?
   b My new _____ is about my latest journey through Madagascar.

2 Writing skill *so, because*

Join the sentences with *so* or *because*.

1. The bus was cancelled. We waited for the next one.
   The bus was cancelled so we waited for the next one.
2. The flight was cancelled. The weather was terrible.
3. The food was hot and spicy. We drank a litre of water with our meal.
4. The meeting was long and boring. The managing director spoke for two hours!
5. The restaurant didn't take credit cards. I paid with cash.
6. The hotel restaurant was closed. We went into the centre of town for a meal.

Writing a description of a journey

3 You write a travel blog. Write a short blog post (80–100 words) about the journey in these pictures.

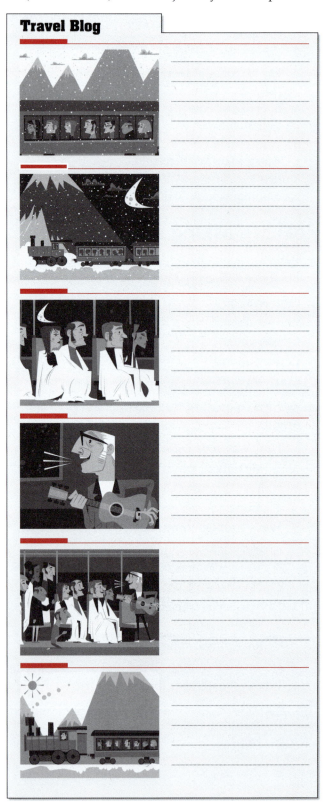

Unit 7 Journeys

Wordbuilding *really/very* + adjective

▶ **WORDBUILDING *really/very* + adjective**

You can make some adjectives stronger or weaker with *really*, *very* or *not very*.

My dinner was really good. (+ +)

My meal was good. (+)

My meal wasn't very good. (– –)

The TV programme was very interesting. (+ +)

The TV programme was interesting. (+)

The TV programme wasn't very interesting. (– –)

You can use *very* and *really* with these adjectives: *good, bad, interesting, comfortable, nice*.

You can only use *really* (not *very*) with these adjectives: *great, amazing, delicious*.

1 Read the sentences and look at the symbols in brackets. Rewrite the sentences using *very* or *really*.

1 The journey was good. (+ +)
   The journey was very/really good.

2 The food wasn't good. (+ +)

3 The meetings were interesting. (– –)

4 The party was great! (+ +)

5 The weather was bad. (+ +)

6 It was sunny. (– –)

7 The meal wasn't very nice. (+ +)

8 The hotel was amazing! (+ +)

Learning skills draw pictures

2 Pictures are a good way to learn new language. Look at these pictures in a learner's notebook. Match the language points (1–3) with the pictures (a–c).

1 opposite adjectives
2 comparative adjectives
3 superlative adjectives

3 Choose eight new words you learned in Unit 7 of the Student's Book. Write them in your notebook and draw pictures to help you remember them.

Check!

4 What is the connection between the names on the left and the numbers on the right? Can you remember? Check your answers in Unit 7 of the Student's Book.

Mayflower and 17th century. They sailed to America in the Mayflower in the 17th century.

1 Mayflower — 30 metres
2 Mayflower II — 35 kilometres
3 Silver Queen — 1977
4 Saiga — 17th century
5 Tree frog — 349,000 kilometres
6 Loggerhead turtle — 1957
7 Voyager — 14,000 kilometres
8 Jupiter — 44 days

Unit 8 Appearance

8a Describing appearance

1 Vocabulary extra adjectives about festivals

Replace the words in bold with these adjectives.

~~boring~~   colourful   crowded   fun   noisy

1 The festival was**n't interesting**.
   boring

2 The musicians and their instruments were very **loud**.

3 The streets were **full of people**.

4 The people's clothes were **lots of different colours**.

5 We had **a good time** at the festival.

Reading the face of Cleopatra

2 Read the article. Are the sentences true (T) or false (F)?

1 When Cleopatra was born, she was the queen.
2 Nowadays, people don't learn about Cleopatra.
3 We don't know what Cleopatra looked like.
4 Archaeologists find objects from Alexandria under the water.
5 There are pictures of Cleopatra under the water.
6 Two thousand years ago, writers often described her appearance.
7 Her face was on coins.
8 It's easy to see her appearance on the coins.

The face of Cleopatra

Cleopatra was born in Egypt over two thousand years ago. She was eighteen when her father died and she became a famous queen. In the modern world, she is still famous. Schoolchildren read about her in books. We watch her in films at the cinema and on TV. In modern pictures and old paintings she is always beautiful.

But what did Cleopatra look like? No one knows exactly. She lived in the ancient city of Alexandria. But over time, a lot of Alexandria disappeared and nowadays most of this region is underwater. Some archaeologists study the objects under the water, but there isn't a face of the queen.

Some historians from the period wrote about the queen. But they describe her power and do not tell us about her appearance. The only real picture of Cleopatra is on some metal coins from Alexandria. One coin shows a woman's face with a large nose. Another coin shows a long neck. But none of the coins are clear, so the face of Cleopatra is still a mystery.

Vocabulary face and appearance

3 Match these words with the parts of the face.

lips _____ ear _____
eyebrow _____ eye _____
cheek _____ chin _____
nose _____

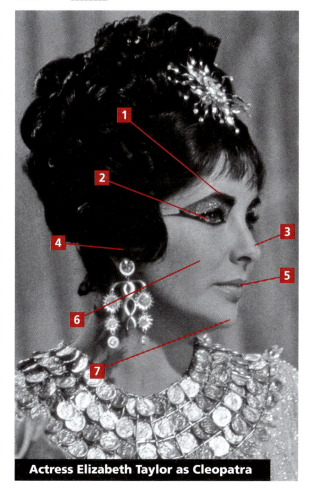

Actress Elizabeth Taylor as Cleopatra

4 Choose the correct option to complete the description of the actress in the photo.

This is a ¹*beautiful / handsome* woman. She's got ²*short / long*, ³*straight / curly* hair. It's ⁴*blonde / dark*.

Grammar have got / has got

5 Complete the description of the photo with these verbs.

| has got (x2) | 's | 're | have got |

I was in Venice last year so I took a lot of photos. At the Venice Carnival, people ¹_____ amazing costumes. They ² _____ always very beautiful. This man ³ _____ a great mask, and his costume ⁴ _____ big blue and gold wings. I think he ⁵ _____ a handsome butterfly!

6 Pronunciation groups of consonants

🔊 **2.7** Listen to these words. Write the missing letters.

1 li_ _
2 eye_ _ow
3 u_ _ _
4 ma_ _
5 _ _ee_ _
6 _ _ _ai_ _ _
7 _ _o_ _e
8 ha_ _ _ome

8b Global fashion

Listening clothes around the world

1 🔊 **2.8** Listen to descriptions of these photos. Match the descriptions (1–5) with the photos (a–e).

Description 1 _____
Description 2 _____
Description 3 _____
Description 4 _____
Description 5 _____

2 🔊 **2.8** Listen again and answer the questions for each description.

Description 1
1 Are the women at work?

2 Which country are they in?

Description 2
3 Which country is the police officer in?

4 Does he work in a city or on a reservation?

Description 3
5 What colours are their clothes?

6 Why is the purple robe good in the mountains of Nepal?

Description 4
7 What colours are Masai clothes?

8 How does the speaker describe the Masai man's hair?

Description 5
9 What is the woman doing on the side of the road?

10 Which clothes does the speaker describe?

Word focus *like*

3 Put the words in order to make sentences with *like*.

1 we   clothes   buying   like   new

2 dress   like   your   is   mine   new

3 my   old   ones   these   shoes   like   are

4 my   uniform   like   I   don't

5 like   a   cowboy   hat   this   hat   is

6 jeans   Jason   wearing   likes

4 Look at the sentences from Exercise 3. Answer the questions.

1 Which sentences use *like* as a verb? _____, _____ and _____

2 Which sentences use *like* with the meaning 'similar to'? _____, _____ and _____

Unit 8 Appearance

Grammar present continuous

5 Look at these pictures. Then complete the sentences with the affirmative or negative present continuous form of the verbs in brackets.

1 He *isn't wearing* (wear) normal clothes.
  He *'s wearing* (wear) a uniform because he's in the army.
2 Trisha _____ (buy) clothes. She _____ (sell) clothes.
3 Georgio _____ (make) a dress. He _____ (design) one.
4 He _____ (play) a computer game. He _____ (read) a book.

6 Use the prompts to write questions for these answers about the pictures in Exercise 5.

1 what / he?
  _____?
  A uniform.
2 Trisha / or / clothes?
  _____?
  She's buying them.
3 what / Georgio?
  _____?
  A dress.
4 play / a computer game?
  _____?
  No, he isn't.

7 Complete the sentences with the present simple or present continuous form of these verbs.

| come | know | learn | like | stand | stay |
| take | walk | | | | |

1 My family _____ from Vietnam.
2 We _____ with friends in Japan for two weeks.
3 I sometimes _____ photos of ordinary people in interesting clothes.
4 Why _____ you _____ here? Let's go!
5 _____ you _____ Peter? Yes, I do. He works in my office.
6 I _____ to work today because the weather is nice.
7 How is your English course? _____ you _____ a lot?
8 _____ you _____ my new shirt? Yes, I do. It's very nice!

Vocabulary clothes

8 Read the clues and complete the crossword with clothes words. What's the mystery word?

1 Wear this on your head.
2 Women wear this.
3 We put on a pair of these and walk outside.
4 Wear this over a shirt so you are warm.
5 At home I wear a T-_____ and at work I wear a _____ and tie.
6 This holds your trousers up!
7 It's like a dress, but it's only the bottom half.
8 Wear these on your feet when it's cold.

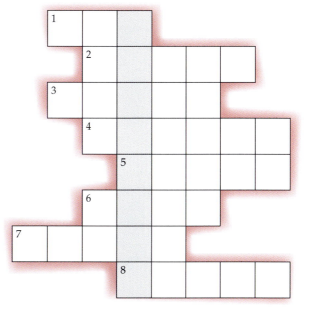

Mystery word: _____

8c Changing your appearance

Listening animal camouflage

1 🔊 2.9 Listen to part of a nature programme about how animals use their appearance. Tick the animals they talk about.

2 🔊 2.9 Listen again. Answer the questions with *Yes*, *No* or *Don't know* (because the speaker doesn't say).

1 Are a lot of animals the same colour as the landscape?
2 Is a deer easy to see in the forest?
3 Are zebras the same colour as the landscape?
4 Are zebras colour blind?
5 Do lions look for one zebra?
6 Are the large, round colours on some butterfly wings like eyes?
7 Does a chameleon change colour for camouflage?
8 Is an Arctic fox white in the autumn?

Vocabulary parts of the body

3 Complete the sentences with these words.

arm	back	foot	hand	knee	leg
neck	shoulder				

1 Kick the ball with your _____.
2 When you meet someone, shake their _____ and say, 'Pleased to meet you.'
3 She's got beautiful jewellery around her _____. Is it gold?
4 You look tired. Lie down on your _____ and go to sleep.
5 Why are you standing on one _____?
6 Carry this bag over your _____.
7 Bend your leg at the _____.
8 Your hand is at the end of your _____.

 1 deer ☐
 2 squirrel ☐
 3 zebra ☐
 4 elephant ☐

 5 lion ☐
 6 butterfly ☐
 7 chameleon ☐
 8 polar bear ☐

 9 Artic fox ☐
 10 giraffe ☐

Glossary

camouflage (n) /ˈkæməˌflɑːʒ/ when animals or humans use or change their appearance so their enemies cannot see them

colour blind (n) /ˈkʌləˌblaɪnd/ when you can't see the difference between some colours

danger (n) /ˈdeɪndʒə/ the possibility that something will hurt you

enemy (n) /ˈenəmi/ a person or an animal that wants to hurt another person or animal

landscape (n) /ˈlændˌskeɪp/ the appearance of the land in a natural area

8d Photos

Real life talking about pictures and photos

1 🔊 **2.10** Listen to a student. She is describing this photo for an English exam. Answer the questions.

1 What does she think the photo shows?

2 What are the children waiting for?

3 Who is looking through a telescope?

4 How does the family look?

5 How does she know they are from Lapland in northern Norway?

2 Complete the description with these phrases.

I think	in front of her	in the middle
on the right	the family looks
the photo is interesting	they are wearing
this photo

¹_____ shows a family, I think. ²_____ is the grandmother and on the left is the mother, maybe. The two children ³_____ are waiting for dinner. The girl is looking at something and, ⁴_____, the boy is looking through a telescope. But I think it's the wrong way round! ⁵_____ serious, but perhaps they are hungry. ⁶_____ special clothes. ⁷_____ they are from Lapland in northern Norway because the women's hats and clothes are from this region. ⁸_____ because it shows people in their everyday life.

3 🔊 **2.10** Listen again and check your answers.

4 Pronunciation silent letters

🔊 **2.11** These letters are silent in some words. Listen to the words (1–8). Which letter is silent?

| b | d | e | h | k | n | t | w |

1 listen   *t*
2 who
3 Wednesday
4 climb
5 what
6 knee
7 blonde
8 autumn

8e How RU? ☺ tks

1 Writing skill textspeak

Match the textspeak with these words or phrases.

2day	CU	@	GR8	atm	4get	b4
l8	pls	:-)	RU	w/e	UR	4u	sry
thx	Weds	<3				

1 your
2 for you
3 see you
4 today
5 before
6 Wednesday
7 at
8 are you
9 great
10 please
11 late
12 sorry
13 thanks
14 love
15 forget
16 at the moment
17 happy
18 weekend

2 Write these sentences using textspeak.

1 Please come on Wednesday.
   pls come on weds

2 Are you happy today?

3 Sorry I'm late.

4 Are we meeting at the weekend?

5 I love the film.

6 I have great news!

7 Call me before you leave.

8 See you later.

Writing texts and online messages

3 Read the situation and write a text message conversation between two friends.

Two friends (A and B) are meeting, but A is on a train and he's late for the meeting. He wants to change the time of the meeting. B is waiting outside a cinema but she wants to meet in a café.

A:

B:

A:

B:

A:

B:

A:

B:

Wordbuilding phrasal verbs

▶ **WORBUILDING phrasal verbs**

A phrasal verb is a verb with a particle. For example:
put + on = put on

take + off = take off

Some phrasal verbs are transitive and some phrasal verbs are intransitive.
- Transitive = verb + particle + something: *Put on your coat.*
- Intransitive = verb + particle: *Get up!*

1 Complete the sentences with these phrasal verbs.

eat out	get up	go back	look at
look up	put on	take off	turn off

1 It's cold outside! _____ your hat and coat!
2 I always _____ at six o'clock and have fruit for breakfast.
3 I'm hungry. Can we _____ at a restaurant tonight?
4 _____ this photo of some people on a train. It's interesting.
5 I can't hear! Please _____ that music!
6 You forgot your homework! _____ and get it.
7 It's hot in here. _____ your coat and hat!
8 You can _____ words in your dictionary.

Learning skills dictionary skills (2)

2 You can look up phrasal verbs in your dictionary. Look at these examples. [T] means the verb is transitive and [I] means the verb is intransitive.

> **put on** /ˌpʊtˈɒn/ [T] to start wearing something
> *She put on her hat and coat and she went outside.*

> **eat out** /ˌiːtˈaʊt/ [I] to have a meal in a restaurant
> *We always eat out at the weekend.*

3 Look at the sentences in Exercise 1. Five of the phrasal verbs are transitive. Three are intransitive. Write T or I. Check your answers in a dictionary.

1 *T (put on)*
2 *I (get up)*
3 _____
4 _____
5 _____
6 _____
7 _____
8 _____

Check!

4 Do the quiz. You can find the answers in Unit 8 of the Student's Book.

1 Where is the Dinagyang Festival?
2 What are the children wearing at the festival in Catalonia?
3 Where can you see a Polga tribesman?
4 Where did archaeologists find a five-thousand-year-old man?
5 What decorations are important in Polynesia?
6 Who wrote the book *Ancient Marks*?
7 Which photographer takes photos of people in their everyday life?
8 What do you call the faces in texts and online messages?

Unit 9 Film and the arts

9a At the cinema

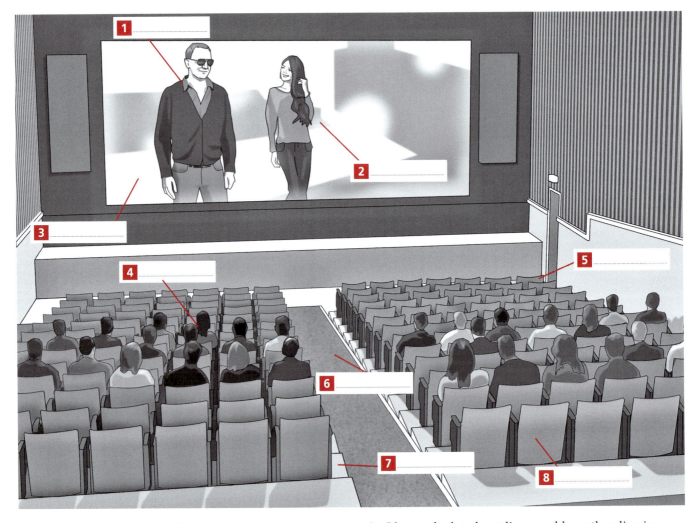

1 Vocabulary extra at the cinema

Label the picture with these words.

| actor | aisle | actress | audience |
| back row | front row | screen | seat |

Vocabulary films

2 Complete the sentences with these types of film.

| animation | comedy | documentary | horror |
| romantic comedy | science fiction | | |

1 *When Harry met Sally* is a famous _____ about two friends. In the end, they fall in love.
2 It's a _____ film about a man. He's driving his car in the middle of the night. Suddenly the engine stops, so he goes into an old house and never returns!
3 I learned a lot about lions and how they live in the wild from the _____.
4 My children love _____ films, especially the ones by Disney.
5 _____ films are usually in space.
6 I like the two actors but I didn't like the film. Normally they are very funny but they weren't in this _____. It was boring and I didn't laugh.

Listening films

3 2.12 Listen to extracts from four different films. Match the films (1–4) with the types of film (a–d).

Film 1   a romantic comedy
Film 2   b documentary
Film 3   c action film
Film 4   d science fiction

4 🔊 **2.12** Listen again. Choose the correct option (a–c) to complete these sentences.

Film 1

1 The mountains are _____.
   a red   b white   c black
2 A _____ is moving fast towards the man.
   a spaceship   b light   c planet

Film 2

3 The animals normally _____ at night.
   a come out   b eat   c sleep
4 The mother is looking for _____.
   a a place to live   b her children
   c food

Film 3

5 _____ says, 'Don't move!'
   a A police officer   b The bank manager
   c The man
6 The man says he didn't take the _____.
   a money   b gold   c credit card

Film 4

7 The woman says she is _____.
   a not bad   b not very well   c fine
8 The man thinks the woman is _____.
   a older   b beautiful
   c older and beautiful

Grammar *going to* (for plans)

5 Match sentences 1–6 with sentences a–f to make pairs.

1 The children are hungry.
2 My brother wants to be a film director.
3 Mike and I like to be near the screen.
4 The book is very good.
5 I need some money.
6 Anousheh has got some money.

a She's going to buy our tickets.
b He's going to Hollywood!
c Steven Spielberg is going to make a film of it.
d They're going to eat lunch.
e We're going to sit in the front row.
f I'm going to get a job.

6 Look at the pictures. Write their plans with *going to* and these verbs.

buy   have   make   meet   play   watch

1 I _____ a film.
2 You _____ tennis.
3 He _____ shoes.
4 She _____ a friend.
5 We _____ dinner.
6 They _____ a film.

7 Pronunciation /tə/

a 🔊 **2.13** Listen to these two sounds: /tə/ and /tuː/.

b 🔊 **2.14** Listen to eight sentences. Tick the sound you hear: /tə/ or /tuː/.

1 /tə/   /tuː/
2 /tə/   /tuː/
3 /tə/   /tuː/
4 /tə/   /tuː/
5 /tə/   /tuː/
6 /tə/   /tuː/
7 /tə/   /tuː/
8 /tə/   /tuː/

9b Film-makers and artists

Vocabulary art and entertainment

1 Complete the diagram with these words. You can use some words more than once.

actor   artist   audience   film   music   musical   musicians
novel   painting   screen   writer

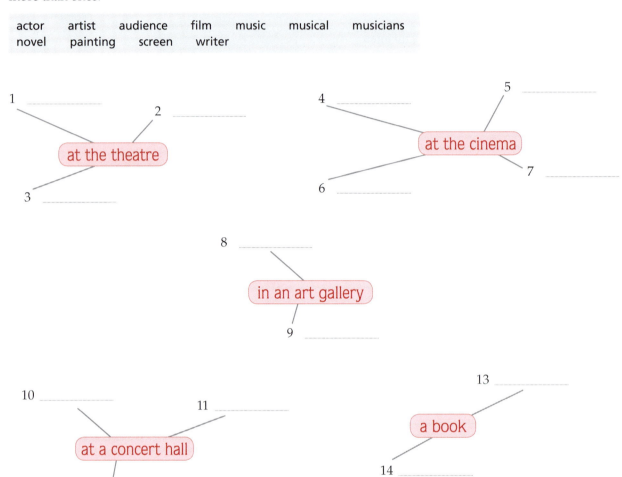

2 Pronunciation word stress

🔊 **2.15** Listen to the stress pattern in these words. Then complete the table with the words.

actresses   artist   cinema   director
gallery   musical   musician   novel
painting   theatre   writer

●•	●••	•●•

Reading an interview with a documentary film-maker

3 Complete the article about the film-maker Bryan Smith with these questions (a–h).

a   What types of film does he make?
b   What are his other interests?
c   How did he become a film-maker?
d   Why does he like adventure film-making?
e   Where does he live?
f   What does he do in his free time?
g   What was his favourite film project?
h   What is his normal day?

Filmmaker: Bryan Smith

1 ....
In a city called Squamish in Canada.

2 ....
He didn't go to film school. He became an adventurer and athlete and then he learned camera skills. He worked with other film-makers and they taught him.

3 ....
Because he loves exploring places and he films the lives of some very interesting people.

4 ....
He doesn't have a normal day.

5 ....
Documentaries. His first film was *49 Megawatts*. He also films adventure sports for *National Geographic*. Next he's going to make a TV series for the Internet about sportspeople.

6 ....
The Kamchatka Project expedition in 2010. It was a wild and remote place.

7 ....
He loves kayaking and skiing.

8 ....
In the film business people don't have much time, so he spends his free time with his family.

Grammar infinitive of purpose

4 Combine phrases from each list to make *I'm going to* + infinitive of purpose sentences.

1 borrow this book — study acting
2 download this song — read about film-making
3 book tickets — listen to it
4 buy this film — watch it later
5 evening classes — learn French
6 drama school — see a play

1 I'm going to *borrow this book*
to *read about film-making*.

2 I'm going to ....
to ....

3 I'm going to ....
to ....

4 I'm going to ....
to ....

5 I'm going to ....
to ....

6 I'm going to ....
to ....

5 Dictation arts news

🔊 **2.16** Listen to and read this article. Complete the article with infinitives of purpose.

Film, music and arts news

We look at the latest news from the world of film, music and art.

Josh Roberts is going to work in Hollywood
1 ....

The young Irish film director is going to buy a house in Los Angeles 2 ....
He said, 'I'm not going there forever.'

The band Stronger are going to be on TV next week 3 ....
Switch on at seven on Wednesday evening
4 .... about the group.

There is going to be an exhibition of Javier Bowman's art at the National Gallery
5 ....

The exhibition opens on 10th January. Phone this number (0845 4785)
6 ....

9c Nature in art

Vocabulary nature

1 Choose the correct option to complete the sentences.

1. I like watching the *birds / butterflies* around the flowers and looking at their coloured wings.
2. The forest has hundreds of tall, old *trees / leaves*.
3. Bananas are a type of *grass / fruit*.
4. Australia is famous for its *kangaroos / polar bears*.
5. We prefer walking in the *rocks / mountains* to walking in the forest.
6. In the autumn the *grass / leaves* fall from the trees.
7. In parts of Australia, some *Rock / Tree* Art is 30,000 years old.
8. Penguins spend a lot of their time in the *sea / sky*.

Listening War Horse

2 🔊 **2.17** Listen to a description of *War Horse*. Number these topics in the order you hear them (1–3).

The play _____ The book _____ The film _____

3 🔊 **2.17** Listen again. Are the sentences true (T) or false (F)?

1. Michael Morpurgo wrote the book in 1982.
2. The book is for adults.
3. The book is about Joey and the First World War.
4. *War Horse* became a stage play in 2007.
5. In the play, they used real horses.
6. You can see the play in different countries.
7. Spielberg used one horse to play Joey in the film version.
8. The film had large audiences.

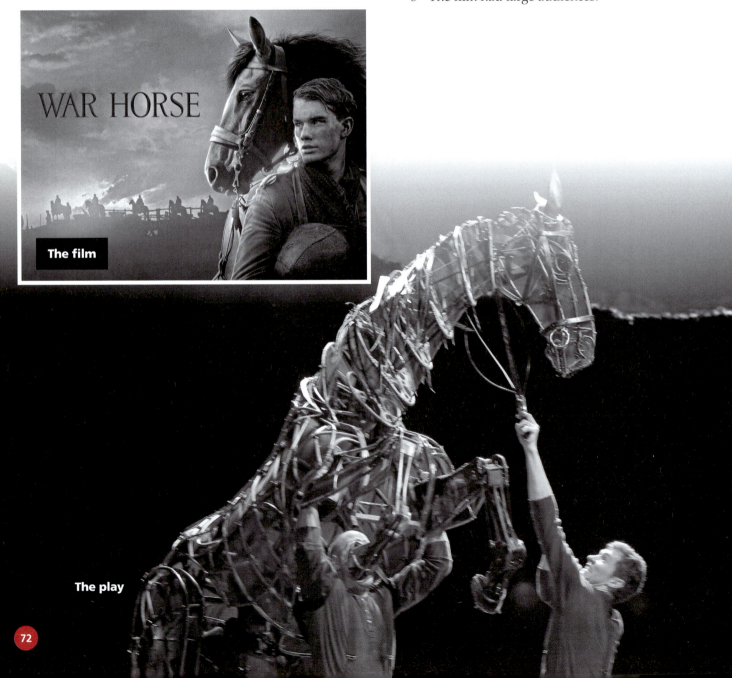

The film

The play

9d Making arrangements

Real life inviting and making arrangements

1 🔊 **2.18** Listen to a telephone conversation between two friends. Answer the questions.

1 Where is Max going?

2 How much are the tickets for the concert?

3 When is the concert?

4 What is Max's problem?

5 What time are they going to meet?

6 Where are they going to meet?

2 🔊 **2.18** Complete the conversation with these phrases. Then listen again and check.

are you	do you want	I'd love	I'm sorry
let's meet	see you	that's	
would you like to			

R = Richard, M = Max

R: Hi Max. It's Richard.

M: Hi Richard. Sorry, but I'm going to a meeting now so I don't have long.

R: OK, it's just that a friend gave me some free tickets for a concert. ¹ _____ to go?

M: What is it?

R: Some music by Mozart.

M: Hmm, I don't know much about classical music.

R: I don't either but it's free, so ² _____ come?

M: OK thanks, ³ _____ to. When is it?

R: Tomorrow night. ⁴ _____ free?

M: ⁵ _____ but I'm working late tomorrow night.

R: What time do you finish?

M: At seven.

R: That's OK. It starts at eight. ⁶ _____ at seven outside your work.

M: ⁷ _____ great. ⁸ _____ at seven.

3 Pronunciation showing enthusiasm

a 🔊 **2.19** Listen to these four phrases for responding to invitations. Which two speakers show enthusiasm in their pronunciation? Which two don't?

1 I'd really like to.   ☺ ☹
2 I'd love to.   ☺ ☹
3 That sounds fantastic.   ☺ ☹
4 That's great.   ☺ ☹

b 🔊 **2.20** Listen to the four phrases again. Each speaker shows enthusiasm. Listen and repeat.

4 Listen and respond responding to invitations

🔊 **2.21** Listen to four invitations. Respond with phrases from Exercise 3.

Grammar present continuous for future reference

5 Complete the sentences with the present continuous form of the verbs.

1 We *'re meeting* (meet) at two this afternoon.
2 Today I _____ (wear) my mother's old dress.
3 They _____ (go) on holiday in June.
4 Where _____ (you / go)? Work doesn't finish until five o'clock.
5 At the moment, she _____ (talk) to someone. Can I help you?
6 I _____ (not take) a holiday this year.
7 He _____ (work) late tonight.
8 We _____ (not play) tennis any more. Jules won the match twenty minutes ago.

6 Do the sentences in Exercise 5 refer to the present (P) or the future (F)?

1 *F*   5 _____
2 *P*   6 _____
3 _____   7 _____
4 _____   8 _____

9e It looks amazing!

1 Grammar extra sense verbs + adjectives

Complete the sentences about the photos with these adjectives.

| beautiful | delicious | loud | very old |
| well | worried | | |

1 He sounds _____ .
2 He looks _____ .
3 I don't feel _____ .
4 It looks _____ .
5 That smells _____ .
6 This dessert tastes _____ !

2 Writing skill giving your opinion with sense verbs

Complete these sentences from different online reviews and comments with sense verbs.

1 In my opinion, the music on their second album _____ no different to their first.
2 I think the food at this new restaurant _____ fantastic!
3 This new horror film is frightening. The audience _____ scared from the beginning to the end.
4 Damien Hirst's new paintings _____ amazing!
5 I think this perfume _____ terrible! Don't put it on!

Writing reviews and comments

3 Write three reviews. Use the notes and write three sentences for each.

1 The Alhambra
new Middle Eastern café
delicious sandwiches
nice mix of old and new furniture
friendly staff

2 War Horse
a play at the theatre
horse looks amazing
interesting story
loud music

3 Digital Hero II
new computer game
graphics look modern
felt bored
no different to Digital Hero I

Unit 9 **Film and the arts**

Wordbuilding suffixes (2)

1 Choose the correct ending to make nouns for jobs or occupations.

1 study — ent / or / ian — *student*
2 music — er / or / ian
3 write — r / ian / tive
4 paint — ent / er / or
5 explore — or / nt / r
6 art — or / ive / ist
7 direct — or / ive / ist
8 manage — nt / r / ian

Learning skills learn from your mistakes

2 Do you often use the wrong word? It's a good idea to write your mistakes in a notebook and write the correct word next to it. Read the page from a student's notebook and write the correct words.

Check!

3 Match these sentences (a–h) with the places on the map (1–10). Check your answers in Unit 9 of the Student's Book.

a There's an outdoor cinema in this harbour.
b Where the Chukchi people live.
c Andõ Hiroshige's paintings show this country.
d It's the location of the film *Grandma*.
e Damien Hirst is the richest artist here.
f The artist Stanislaw Witkiewicz was born here.
g It's the location of the film *My Wedding and Other Secrets*.
h Adrian Seymour is going to make his next film here.

My mistakes

watching
1 I like ~~seeing~~ TV.

2 Can we ~~hear~~ to the radio?

3 The film is ~~at~~ Friday.

4 We're going to meet ~~on~~ the cinema.

5 How ~~many~~ money is a ticket for the concert?

6 Hamlet is a ~~theatre~~ by William Shakespeare.

7 This novel is very ~~interested~~.

8 The actor Daniel Craig is a ~~beautiful~~ man.

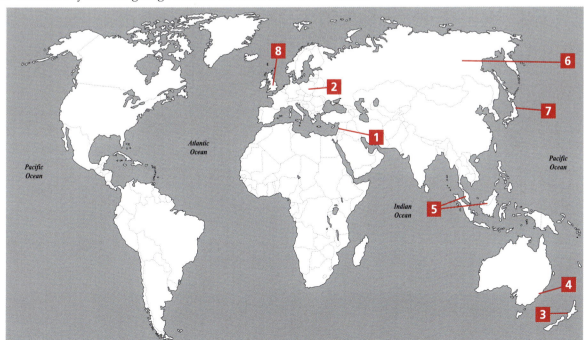

Unit 10 Science

10a Science and technology

Vocabulary science subjects

1 Label the pictures with the types of science.

| astronomy | biology | chemistry | physics |
| neuroscience | technology | zoology |

1 ....

2 ....

3 ....

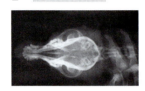
4 ....

5 ....

6 ....

7 ....

Reading science articles

2 Read these extracts from five science articles. Match the extracts (1–5) with the types of science from Exercise 1.

1 ....
With the problem of energy on Earth, some scientists have studied lightning because they want to use the energy in lightning. A single lightning bolt has around five billion joules of energy. Unfortunately, a lightning bolt lasts for seconds, so how do you catch the energy?

2 ....
On the 18th of this month, Mars will be below the Moon and to the right. If it's a clear night, you'll see the red planet without a telescope. It could be the best view this year.

3 ....
We've had PCs, laptops and tablets, so what's next? One team of scientists wants to develop a keyboard on your body. A small device projects the keyboard onto your arm and you type onto your skin.

4 ....
The Durrell Wildlife Conservation Trust is on the island of Jersey. There are a lot of rare animals in the park, but the Trust also gives money to projects with animals in places such as the Galapagos Islands, India, Madagascar and the Caribbean Islands.

5 ....
Mirror neurons help animals to learn. For example, when a young animal watches its mother, it learns how to do something. Scientists believe this is because the mirror neurons in its brain are working.

Vocabulary everyday technology

3 Complete the pairs of sentences with these words.

1 download / CD
   a Listen to this .... from the Internet.
   b I bought a new .... in town last week.

2 search engine / library
   a My father still takes books out of the ....
   b It's quicker to find articles on this topic with a ....

3 map / sat nav
   a Can you open the .... and have a look for the town?
   b Switch on the .... and type in the location.

4 radio / podcast
   a I've downloaded this .... for you to listen to.
   b Turn up the .... The news is on.

5 text / send
   a I've got my phone with me so you can .... me.
   b Why didn't you .... me a postcard while you were on holiday?

Listening explaining technology

4 🔊 **2.22** It's Karen's first day in a new job. Her manager helps her with some technology. Match the conversations (1–3) with the technologies (a–c).

Conversation 1 ......
Conversation 2 ......
Conversation 3 ......

a tablet computer

b answering machine

c photocopier

Grammar present perfect

5 🔊 **2.22** Complete the conversations with the present perfect form of the verbs or *have/haven't*. Then listen again and check your answers.

M = Manager, K = Karen

Conversation 1

M: OK, Karen. ¹.................................. (you ever use) this machine before?

K: Yes, of course I ² .... (use) one before.

M: No, I mean, ³ .... (you ever make) copies with this type of machine? It's different from others.

K: Oh, I see. No, I ⁴ ...., but it looks similar to the one in my previous job.

Conversation 2

M: And this is yours.

K: Oh, I ⁵ .... (never see) one like this before.

M: It's very easy. Press this button.

K: OK. I ⁶ .... (do) that.

M: Great. Has the screen come on?

K: Yes, it ⁷ ....

M: Now you put your finger on the screen.

Conversation 3

K: Someone ⁸ .... (leave) a message on my phone.

M: OK. Press play.

K: I ⁹ .... (press) play but it doesn't work.

M: ¹⁰ .... (you switch) it on?

K: Ah. Sorry! No, I ¹¹ ....

6 Listen and respond *Yes, I have / No, I haven't*

🔊 **2.23** Listen to six *Have you ever …?* questions. Respond with *Yes, I have* or *No, I haven't*.

> Have you ever listened to a podcast?

7 Pronunciation *'ve / 's*

🔊 **2.24** Listen and circle the number of words in each sentence. A contracted form with *'ve* or *'s* is one word (e.g. *I've* or *she's* = one word).

a 3 ④ 5   e 3 4 5
b 3 4 5   f 3 4 5
c 3 4 5   g 3 4 5
d 3 4 5   h 3 4 5

8 Dictation

🔊 **2.24** Listen again and write the sentences.

a *I've printed the photos.*
b ......
c ......
d ......
e ......
f ......
g ......
h ......

77

10b Memory and language

Reading London taxi drivers' memories

1 These sentences are missing from the end of the paragraphs in the article. Match the sentences (a–d) with the paragraphs (1–4).

a They can only use the map inside their head.
b That's because taxi drivers in London have memorised the whole city.
c Scientists believe their training for 'The Knowledge' is the reason for changing their brains.
d For 150 years, they have had to pass this test to become a taxi driver.

2 Read the article again and answer the questions.

1 According to the article, what are the two reasons why London is famous?
  Reason 1: ....
  Reason 2: ....
2 Why is it easier to travel round London in a taxi?
  ....
3 When did London taxi drivers first take the test?
  ....
4 How long does it take to learn 'The Knowledge'?
  ....
5 Can they use technology to answer the questions on the test? Yes / No
6 Can they use a map? Yes / No
7 Which part of the taxi driver's brain have scientists studied? What does it do?
  ....
8 How is the hippocampus different in London taxi drivers' brains?
  ....

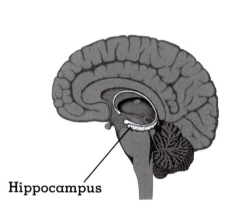
Hippocampus

London is famous as a historic city with lots of interesting places to visit. It's also famous for difficult roads. Tourists and visitors to London quickly become lost in the old streets – even with a map or sat nav. It's much easier to catch a taxi. ¹

Since 1865, trainee London taxi drivers have studied for a test called 'The Knowledge'. They have learned the names of every street, the location of every police station and the fastest route to every theatre. ² ....

Learning 'The Knowledge' can take over two years. When they think they are ready, taxi drivers take the test. They answer questions such as 'What's the fastest route from Buckingham Palace to London University?' They can't use a map or a sat nav. ³ ....

Scientists at London University have studied the brains of London taxi drivers. In particular, they have looked at the part of the brain called the hippocampus. It's the part that stores memories. In London taxi drivers, the hippocampus is bigger than in the brains of other people. ⁴ ....

Unit 10 Science

Vocabulary memory and learning

3 Choose the correct word (a–c) to complete the list of tips for studying for exams.

FIVE TIPS FOR EXAM SUCCESS

- Plan a timetable for studying. Write down the date of the exam and then write the times and days you are going to ¹_____ before it.
- ²_____ short lists of information over short periods of time. Take regular breaks.
- Which things do you often ³_____? Write down that information and study that the most.
- Work with a friend. ⁴_____ each other with questions.
- Don't study the night before. ⁵_____ in the evening and go to bed early.

1 a study   b know   c teach
2 a Forget   b Practise   c Memorise
3 a forget   b know   c train
4 a Memorise   b Learn   c Test
5 a Understand   b Relax   c Remember

Grammar present perfect and past simple

> ▶ SPELL CHECK past simple and past participles
>
> With regular verbs, you add -ed (or -d/-ied) to the end of a verb to make the past simple form or the past participle (see also Unit 6):
>
> | Infinitive | Past simple | Past participle |
> |---|---|---|
> | train | trained | trained |
> | study | studied | studied |
>
> However, irregular verbs have irregular forms. Sometimes the past simple and the past participle have the same irregular form:
>
> | Infinitive | Past simple | Past participle |
> |---|---|---|
> | have | had | had |
> | teach | taught | taught |
>
> Sometimes the past simple and the past participle do not have the same irregular form:
>
> | Infinitive | Past simple | Past participle |
> |---|---|---|
> | know | knew | known |
> | take | took | taken |

4 Complete the table of irregular verbs. You can find the answers in Unit 10 of the Student's Book.

Infinitive	Past simple	Past participle
¹_____	bought	²_____
pay	³_____	paid
⁴_____	put	⁵_____
send	⁶_____	sent
⁷_____	forgot	forgotten
make	⁸_____	made
read	read	⁹_____
¹⁰_____	won	won

5 Complete these sentences with the correct form of the verbs from Exercise 4.

1 Have you ever _____ any books in other languages?
2 Nelson Dellis _____ the Memory Championships in 2010 and 2011.
3 When did you _____ these tickets?
4 Did you _____ me a text or an email?
5 I've _____ the advert for the car in the local newspaper.
6 Have you ever _____ for something with online banking?
7 We've _____ the rule for the present perfect. Can you remind us?

6 Complete these short conversations. Use the same verb twice.

1 take
   A: _Have_ you ever _taken_ an English exam?
   B: Yes, I _took_ one last year.
2 study
   A: _____ you ever _____ Spanish?
   B: Yes, I _____ it when I was a student at university.
3 teach
   A: _____ you ever _____ a subject?
   B: Not exactly, but I _____ a friend how to use his new computer.
4 learn
   A: _____ you ever _____ a musical instrument?
   B: Yes, I _____ the violin at school.
5 write
   A: _____ you ever _____ a book?
   B: No, but I _____ a travel blog when I went round the world.

10c Inventions

Vocabulary science and inventions

1 Write the names of these inventions.

1 i...........

2 v............ c............

3 w...........

4 k...........

5 e...........

6 s........... t...........

7 f...........

8 the I...........

2 Match the descriptions (a–h) with the inventions (1–8) from Exercise 1.

a It turns.
b It plays music.
c It sticks paper.
d It burns.
e It cleans the house.
f It gives energy.
g It cuts.
h It searches for links.

Listening a TV quiz

3 🔊 2.25 Listen to a radio quiz programme. The host asks three questions. Match the questions with the answers (a–c).

First question ....
Second question ....
Third question ....

a Morse Code

b Compass

c Marconi

4 🔊 2.25 Listen again and answer the questions.

1 How many points do the two teams have at the beginning of round five?

2 When did Marconi send a radio message across the Atlantic Ocean?

3 What is the difference between the sounds in Morse Code?

4 When did the Chinese invent the compass?

5 Where did it point?

6 Does the Green team or the Blue team answer the third question correctly?

7 How many points does the Blue team have?

8 How many points does the Green team have?

10d On the phone

Real life checking and clarifying

1 🔊 **2.26** Listen to a telephone conversation. Choose the correct option (a–c) to complete the sentences.

1 The name of the company is _____ Technologies.
   a AGA   b EGA   c AGI
2 Sophie is at the Science Fair in _____.
   a Casablanca   b Cairo   c Cologne
3 The name of the hotel is _____.
   a Insel   b Ensal   c Insal
4 The number is _____.
   a 021 8843 50   b 021 8834 50   c 021 4508 83
5 Sophie wants the new _____.
   a designs   b prices   c machines

2 🔊 **2.26** Complete the conversation (1–8) with the questions (a–h). Then listen again and check.

a Was that zero two one, eight eight three four, five zero?
b What time is it there?
c Have you emailed me a copy of the new prices?
d Is that six in the morning?
e Was that the Ensal Hotel?
f Can you fax it to the hotel?
g Where are you now?
h Is there anything else?

L = Lance, S = Sophie
L: Hello, AGA Technologies. Can I help you?
S: Hello, Lance. This is Sophie.
L: Hello, Sophie. ¹ _____
S: I'm at the Science Fair in Cologne.
L: Great. ² _____
S: Err, it's six o'clock.
L: ³ _____
S: No, in the evening. I want to give you the name of my hotel for the next two days. It's the Insel Hotel …
L: One moment. I need a pen. OK. ⁴ _____
S: No, the Insel Hotel. I for Italy, N – S – E for England, L.
L: Oh sorry. Insel.
S: And the number is zero two one, eight eight three four, five zero.
L: ⁵ _____
S: That's right.
L: ⁶ _____
S: ⁷ _____
L: No, I haven't because your email wasn't working.
S: That's strange. ⁸ _____ I don't know the number.
L: Don't worry. I've just looked at your hotel website and there's a fax number on that.
S: Great, thank you. I'll call you later. Bye for now.

3 Pronunciation contrastive stress

a Read these five conversations. Which word do you think B stresses? Underline it.

1 A: Is that two in the morning?
   B: No, it's three in the morning.
2 A: Was that the Ensel Hotel?
   B: No, it was the Insel Hotel.
3 A: Is that I for Italy?
   B: No, it's A for Amsterdam.
4 A: Is that two in the morning?
   B: No, it's two in the afternoon.
5 A: Was that three double six?
   B: No, it was three double seven.

b 🔊 **2.27** Listen and check your answers.

10e Telephone messages

Vocabulary email addresses and websites

1 Match the parts of the email addresses and websites with the words.

1	@		dot com
2	.com		at
3	/		dash
4	-		dot co dot uk
5	www.		dot org
6	//		underscore
7	:		double slash
8	.org		slash
9	_		www dot
10	.co.uk		colon

2 Read the words of three people saying email addresses and websites. Write the address or website.

1. *So that's h underscore schmitt at hotmail dot co dot de.*

2. *The hotel website is www dot concordia dot com.*

3. *Download the podcast from www dot instolisten dot org slash dailypod dash 2*

3 Writing skill imperatives

Read the speakers' words. Rewrite the sentences so they start with an imperative.

1. Can you call Stacey back?
   Call Stacey back.

2. I'd like you to send everyone a letter.

3. Can you take Mr D'Souza to the station?

4. Would you book a table for two?

5. Can you buy more paper?

6. Would you print these photographs, please?

7. Can you email the designs to g_rich@gmail.com?

8. I'd like you to telephone the hotel.

Writing a telephone message

4 🔊 2.28 Listen to three voicemails. Complete the messages.

1
MESSAGE
Name of caller: _____
Message for: _____
Message: _____
_____
_____
_____
Urgent _____

2
MESSAGE
Name of caller: _____
Message for: _____
Message: _____
_____
_____
_____
Urgent _____

3
MESSAGE
Name of caller: _____
Message for: _____
Message: _____
_____
_____
_____
Urgent _____

Wordbuilding synonyms and antonyms

1 Replace the words in bold with a synonym.

> call   find   memorise   search   send
> show   stop working   study

1 Please **email** me the photographs.
2 **Read** the grammar rules.
3 Look at this list of words. How many can you **learn and remember**?
4 **Look** for the answer to this question on the Internet.
5 Can you **teach** me how to use the photocopier?
6 Scientists need to **discover** the answer.
7 Did you **telephone** the cinema for film times?
8 Robots often **break down**.

2 Complete these pairs of sentences with the correct antonym.

1 remember / forget
   a I always _____ the Chinese word for 'house'.
   b Can you _____ the Chinese word for 'house'?

2 leave / take
   a Eduardo is out of the office. Do you want me to _____ a message?
   b Eduardo is out of the office. Do you want to _____ a message for him?

3 teach / learn
   a You're good at playing the guitar! Can you _____ me?
   b I'd like to _____ how to play the guitar.

4 send / receive
   a Did we _____ any emails from any customers today?
   b Did you _____ the contracts to our customers?

Learning skills your learning style

3 Students can have different learning styles. Some students are more:
- Visual (They learn by looking.)
- Auditory (They learn by listening.)
- Kinaesthetic (They learn by doing.)

Do this quiz to find out your learning style. Choose the best ending (a–c) for you to complete these sentences.

What's your learning style?

1 When I learn English in class,
   a I like watching the teacher.
   b I like listening to the teacher.
   c I like doing something with other people.

2 When I learn a new word,
   a I draw a picture of it.
   b I repeat the word many times.
   c I imagine it in my head.

3 When I study for an English test,
   a I write notes and use different colours.
   b I talk to myself or other people about my notes.
   c I study and do physical activity at the same time.

What do your answers mean?

Mostly A answers = You are a visual learner.
Mostly B answers = You are an auditory learner.
Mostly C answers = You are a kinaesthetic learner.

Check!

4 Answer the questions. You can check your answers in Unit 10 of the Student's Book.

a What are three words ending with -*ology*?
   1 _____ology
   2 _____ology
   3 _____ology

b What are three ways to send information?
   1
   2
   3

c What three types of new technology do you use every day?
   1
   2
   3

d What three old inventions do you never use?
   1
   2
   3

Unit 11 Tourism

11a Holiday advice

1 Vocabulary extra types of holiday

Put the letters in order to make types of holiday.
1 NGCMAPI
2 SISENEGHTIG
3 BKANACKPCIG
4 KIINGH

Vocabulary tourism

2 Replace the words in bold with these words.

book	carry on	check in	rent
return ticket	sightseeing	souvenirs	
tour guide			

1 I'd like a **ticket to take me there and back**.
   return ticket
2 Let's go **and look at some of the famous places in the city**.
3 I have one bag to **put on the plane** and one **bag to take on the plane**.
4 When we land at the airport we could **pay money to have** a car for the week.
5 The **person who showed us round the city** knew a lot of history and could answer all our questions.
6 I bought some **nice objects connected with the city** to give to family and friends at home.
7 Did you **telephone the hotel in advance for** a room?

Reading Doug Lansky

3 Read the article about travel writer Doug Lansky. Answer the questions with *Yes, No* or *Don't know* (because the information isn't in the article).

1 Does Doug still travel nowadays?
2 Does he write for travel magazines?
3 Does he take a backpack?
4 Does he like travelling with other people?
5 Does he often go sightseeing?
6 Does he like meeting local people?
7 Are the photos on his site from all over the world?
8 Can you put any type of travel photo on his website?

Alternative travel

Doug Lansky started travelling when he was young and, as an adult, he never stopped. He's travelled all over the world and he writes about his experiences for magazines. He also writes travel guide books.

Doug doesn't go to places with lots of tourists and he hates travelling with other 'travellers'. He likes to visit new places and spend a lot of time there and meet the local people. He also takes hundreds of photos. In particular, he photographs signs around the world because he thinks they are more interesting than normal travel photos. This was his first photo of a sign:

Now he has a website called www.signspotting.com with hundreds of signs from different countries. Tourists and travellers put up their favourite signs from around the world. The photographs don't have to be great, but they have to be interesting and funny.

Doug Lansky

Word focus *take*

4 Match the sentence beginnings (1–5) with the endings (a–e).

1. I want a photo of us in front of the Eiffel Tower. Can you take
2. We're late for our flight. Let's take
3. I'm so tired of working. It's time to take
4. You're wet! Why didn't you take
5. We don't speak Spanish so we should take
6. The only way to the Antarctic is to take

a a cruise.
b your camera with you on holiday?
c your umbrella?
d a phrase book.
e a taxi to the airport. It's faster.
f a very long holiday!

Grammar *should/shouldn't*

5 Choose the correct options to complete these sentences.

1. You *should / shouldn't* buy them!
2. You *should / shouldn't* stay there.
3. You *should / shouldn't* go home.
4. You *should / shouldn't* come here on holiday.
5. You *should / shouldn't* watch TV all day!
6. You *should / shouldn't* take a photo.

6 Correct the mistake in each sentence.

1. You should to book a hotel room.
   You should book a hotel room.
2. He doesn't should work late.
3. Do we should buy a ticket here?
4. She shoulds check in her bag.
5. You don't should rent a car.
6. What should we to eat?

Writing email advice to a friend

7 You have received this email from a friend. Underline the advice he asks for.

Hi!
I've booked my tickets and I'm arriving on the 21st! Before I arrive at your house, I'm going to travel round the country. Should I rent a car or go by public transport, do you think? Also I'm going to spend some time in the capital. What should I see there? And should I book my hotel in advance? Can you give me any advice? Oh! And what's the weather like? Is it cold? Should I bring lots of clothes?
See you soon!
Mike ☺

8 Write a reply to Mike. Complete this email.

Dear Mike

I'm really happy that you are coming to my country.

Here is my advice:

When you travel round the country, you should

In my capital city, you should

For hotels, I think you should

At the moment the weather is very cold, so you should

See you soon!

11b Planning a holiday

Listening advice about holidays

1 🔊 **2.29** Listen to six tourists talking about travel in different countries. Match the tourists (1–5) with the topics (a–f).

Tourist 1 _____
Tourist 2 _____
Tourist 3 _____
Tourist 4 _____
Tourist 5 _____
Tourist 6 _____

a road travel
b weather
c money and currency
d language
e safety and emergencies
f visas and immigration

2 🔊 **2.29** Listen again. Answer the questions for each tourist.

Tourist 1
1 What type of transport did he take?

2 Did he pay for medical costs?

Tourist 2
3 Which part of the world does she talk about?

4 What clothes does she suggest?

Tourist 3
5 Which country did he go to?

6 Why was road travel difficult?

Tourist 4
7 Who needs a visa to stay longer than three months in the USA?

8 Who should you contact for a work visa?

Tourist 5
9 What did he take to Mexico?

10 Where did he need it?

Tourist 6
11 Does she change money before or after she arrives in a country?

12 When does she use her credit card?

Vocabulary in another country

3 Read the clues and complete the crossword.

Across
1 The _____ is hot in the south, but colder in the north.
3 Get a _____ from the embassy before you go.
5 Russia has nine different time _____.
6 You need a driving _____ to drive a car.
7 London is a multi-_____ city with people from all over the world.

Down
1 The _____ in Canada is the dollar.
2 Drive on the left-_____ side in the UK, Australia, Japan, Ireland and Kenya.
4 It's _____ to travel without a passport.

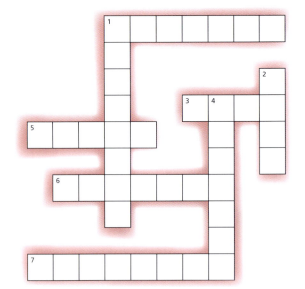

Grammar *have to / don't have to, can/can't*

4 Choose the correct option (a–c) to complete the information from an airline website.

1. a have to   b have   c don't have to
2. a can't   b don't have to   c can
3. a can   b can't   c have to
4. a have to   b can't   c don't have to
5. a have to   b don't have to   c can't
6. a can   b can to   c have
7. a don't have to b can't   c have to
8. a can   b can't   c have to

5 Dictation travel announcements

🔊 **2.30** Listen to four announcements at an airport and complete the sentences.

1. All passengers on _____ Gate 13 immediately.
2. _____ liquids over one hundred millilitres _____ .
3. Passengers _____ this line.
4. Adults _____ first.

6 Pronunciation / hæftə/

🔊 **2.31** Listen to six sentences with the words *have to*. Tick the pronunciation you hear.

1. /hæftə/ ✓   /hæf tuː/
2. /hæftə/   /hæf tuː/
3. /hæftə/   /hæf tuː/
4. /hæftə/   /hæf tuː/
5. /hæftə/   /hæf tuː/
6. /hæftə/   /hæf tuː/

Information for passengers

→ You ¹_____ check in before going through security. You ²_____ do this online or at the airport.

→ You ³_____ take carry-on bags over 10 kg on to the plane. Check these in before you fly.

→ Passengers flying to airports in the same country ⁴_____ show a passport but you must show some form of ID.

→ Passengers travelling to foreign countries ⁵_____ travel without a valid passport.

→ On some flights, you ⁶_____ pay extra to change your seat to one in business class.

→ You ⁷_____ use mobile phones and electronic devices when the plane is taking off and landing.

→ When the seatbelt sign is off, passengers ⁸_____ get up from their seat.

11c Being polite in other countries

Listening customs in other countries

1 🔊 **2.32** Listen to a radio programme about how to be polite in other countries. Which two countries do they talk about?

2 🔊 **2.32** Listen again. Read and tick *Do* or *Don't* for the two countries.

	DO	DON'T
First country		
1 Shake hands when you meet people.		
2 Take flowers to someone's house.		
3 Wear your shoes in someone's house.		
4 Join in the dancing.		
Second country		
5 Eat before the oldest person at the table.		
6 Cross your chopsticks.		
7 Shake hands or bow when you meet someone.		
8 Take flowers to someone's house.		

Grammar *everywhere, somewhere, nowhere, anywhere*

3 Complete the sentences with *where*, *thing* or *body*. Use each word twice.

1 Are you doing any_____ interesting this weekend?
2 I put my passport some_____, but I can't find it now.
3 There's some_____ at the door. I don't who it is.
4 Let's go shopping. There's no_____ to eat in the fridge.
5 Every_____ is here so let's have dinner.
6 Are you going any_____ nice for your holiday this year?
7 I'm so bored! Suggest some_____ to do.
8 I invited some friends for dinner but no_____ could come.

4 Choose the correct option to complete these sentences.

1 I don't know *anybody* / *somebody* in the room. Who are they?
2 I'd like *everything* / *something* to drink.
3 There's *everywhere* / *nowhere* like home.
4 *Everything* / *Something* on the menu looks delicious! I want to eat it all!
5 Let's go to a nightclub because *anybody* / *everybody* likes dancing.
6 Let's go *nowhere* / *somewhere* for lunch. How about that new restaurant on the corner?
7 *Somebody* / *Nobody* telephoned earlier but they didn't leave their name.
8 Did *anything* / *everything* happen while I was away?

11d A holiday in Morocco

Listening holiday plans

1 🔊 **2.33** Listen to a conversation between Marie and Enzo. Are the sentences true (T) or false (F)?

1. Marie has booked her holiday this year.
2. Marie wants to go somewhere hot.
3. Enzo suggests Morocco.
4. Marie doesn't think it's a good idea.
5. Marie wants to meet other people.
6. Enzo suggests a tour.
7. Enzo thinks a tour is expensive.
8. Enzo suggests a camping holiday.

Real life making suggestions

2 Put the words in order to make suggestions.

1. can   suggestion   make   I   a   ?

2. go   to   should   you   Morocco

3. you   own   could   on   your   travel

4. why   tour   go   with   don't   you   a   ?

5. going   about   how   on   a   package   holiday   ?

3 🔊 **2.33** Listen to the conversation again and match the suggestions (2–5) from Exercise 2 with these responses (a–c).

a. Maybe you're right.
b. But the disadvantage is that it's more expensive.
c. That's a really good idea.
d. Yes, but I'd like to meet people as well.

4 Listen and respond responding to suggestions

🔊 **2.34** Listen to four suggestions. Respond with a phrase from Exercise 3. Then compare your responses with the model answer that follows.

Why don't you travel on your own?

Yes, but I'd like to meet people as well.

5 Pronunciation /ʌ/, /ʊ/ or /uː/

🔊 **2.35** Listen to these words. Tick the vowel sound you hear: /ʌ/, /ʊ/ or /uː/.

		/ʌ/	/ʊ/	/uː/
1	bus	/ʌ/	/ʊ/	/uː/
2	book	/ʌ/	/ʊ/	/uː/
3	you	/ʌ/	/ʊ/	/uː/
4	but	/ʌ/	/ʊ/	/uː/
5	should	/ʌ/	/ʊ/	/uː/
6	food	/ʌ/	/ʊ/	/uː/
7	cruise	/ʌ/	/ʊ/	/uː/
8	could	/ʌ/	/ʊ/	/uː/

11e Your feedback

1 Writing skill closed and open questions

a Complete the questions with these words.

~~Did~~	What	How many	Was
Were	How	Why	Would

1. _____Did_____ you use room service?
2. _____ the food of a high standard?
3. _____ nights did you stay at the hotel?
4. _____ easy was it to park near the airport?
5. _____ you recommend this sports centre to friends?
6. _____ our staff friendly and polite?
7. _____ other suggestions can you make?
8. _____ did you choose our restaurant?

b Match the questions (1–8) from Exercise 1 with these responses (a–h).

a Two.
b No, I didn't.
c It was very easy.
d Yes, fairly high.
e Yes, I would.
f Because of the location and I like Chinese food.
g Yes, they were.
h You should have a car park at the hotel.

Writing a feedback form

2 The local tourist office in your town has this feedback form for tourists. You are a tourist. Fill in the form with your feedback. Answer the questions and write comments.

Tourist Information

1 How helpful were the staff at our tourist information office?
Very helpful and polite ☐   Helpful and polite ☐
Not helpful or polite ☐
Comment:
_____
_____

2 Did you visit the local historic places? Yes / No
If yes, please comment:
_____
If no, please say why not:
_____

3 Which hotel did you stay at? Please comment on its level of service.
_____
_____

4 Which restaurant(s) did you eat at? Please comment on the quality of the food.
_____
_____

5 Overall, how was your experience of our town?
Excellent ☐   Very good ☐   OK ☐
Not very good ☐
Comment:
_____
_____

6 Would you recommend our town as a tourist destination? Yes / No
If yes, please comment:
_____
If no, please say why not:
_____

Wordbuilding word forms (1)

1 Complete this table of word forms. Use a dictionary to help you.

Verb	Noun	Person
manage	management	¹
photograph	²	³
⁴	study	student
backpack	backpack	⁵
visit	⁶	⁷
⁸	cooker	cook
⁹	design	¹⁰

2 Complete these sentences with words from the table in Exercise 1.

1 I work for a travel company and I _____ six people.
2 I took this great _____ when I was on holiday.
3 When I was a _____ I studied tourism.
4 I can put everything in my _____ when I go on holiday.
5 When you are a _____ in another country, you should learn their language.
6 Don't forget to switch off the _____ in the kitchen.
7 My sister is a fashion _____ for Gucci.

Learning skill pronunciation

3 When you learn a new word, remember to answer these questions about the pronunciation.
- How many syllables are there?
- Where is the main stress?
- Does the pronunciation change with other word forms?

Example:
<u>ma</u>nage (two syllables)   <u>ma</u>nagement (three syllables)   <u>ma</u>nager (three syllables)

Look at the other words in Exercise 1. Write the number of syllables and mark the stressed syllable.

Check!

4 Match these comments from tourists (1–6) with the suggestions (a–f). You can find all the places in Unit 11 of the Student's Book.

1 'I want to see buildings from the Renaissance.'
2 'I'd like to walk through the jungle.'
3 'We're going hiking in the Andes.'
4 'I've never seen the desert.'
5 'I'd like to see Ayers Rock.'
6 'I want to go somewhere with nobody living there.'

You should go to …

a Malaysia
b Florence in Italy
c Jordan
d Australia
e Antarctica
f South America

Unit 12 The Earth

12a Earth trends

1 Vocabulary extra the Earth

Label the diagram with these words.

Antarctic Circle	Arctic Circle	Equator
North Pole	Northern hemisphere	
South Pole	Southern hemisphere	

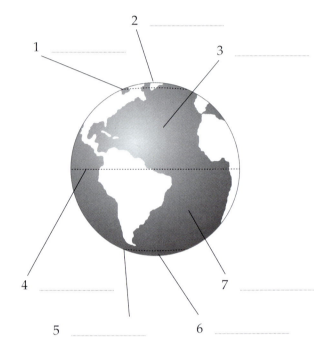

Vocabulary measurements

2 Match the sentence beginnings (1–5) with the endings (a–e).

1 The area of Antarctica is
2 Water becomes ice at a temperature below zero
3 The average adult should drink
4 Thirty per cent
5 The height of the tallest tree on Earth is
6 The weight of the International Space Station (ISS) is

a of the Earth's surface is dry land.
b degrees Celsius.
c fourteen million square kilometres.
d four hundred and nineteen thousand, four hundred and fifty-five kilograms.
e two point five litres of water per day.
f one hundred and thirty metres.

3 Write the measurements in Exercise 2 as numbers and abbreviations.

1 The area of Antarctica: _14,000,000 km²_
2 When water becomes ice: below _____
3 Amount of water for an average adult: _____
4 Earth covered by dry land: _____
5 Height of the tallest tree: _____
6 Weight of the ISS: _____

Listening Earth trends

4 🔊 **2.36** Listen to four predictions of future trends on Earth. Match the predictions (1–4) with the topics (a–e). There is one extra topic.

Prediction 1 _____
Prediction 2 _____
Prediction 3 _____
Prediction 4 _____

a population
b food and water
c energy
d technology
e travel and tourism

International Space Station

5 🔊 **2.36** Listen again. Choose the correct option (a–c) to complete these sentences.

1. Experts think immigration will _____.
   a increase   b decrease
   c stay the same
2. Tourist destinations and popular cities will have problems because there will be so many _____.
   a immigrants   b tourists
   c experts
3. More people live in cities than live in _____.
   a houses   b towns
   c the countryside
4. By 2030 there will be _____ people on the planet.
   a seven billion   b eight billion
   c nine billion
5. Computers and communication across the Earth have increased in the past _____.
   a 50 years   b 40 years
   c 30 years
6. The speed of the technology will _____.
   a become faster   b become slower
   c stay the same
7. Farmers need more _____ to grow food.
   a money   b workers
   c land
8. Many experts are _____ about the future for modern farming.
   a positive   b unhappy
   c worried

Grammar *will/won't*

6 Look at the trends for a small town in England. Write sentences with *will/won't*.

Number of cars

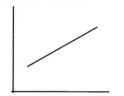

1. The number of ___*cars will*___ increase.

Number of houses

2. The number of _____ stay the same.

Number of children

3. The number of _____ increase.

Temperature in the summer

4. The temperature in _____ decrease.

Rainfall in the winter

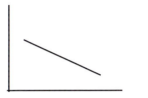

5. The rainfall in _____ decrease.

Number of people

6. The number of _____ increase.

7 Pronunciation *'ll* or *will*

🔊 **2.37** Listen to eight sentences. Do you hear *'ll* or *will*?

1. 'll   will
2. 'll   will
3. 'll   will
4. 'll   will
5. 'll   will
6. 'll   will
7. 'll   will
8. 'll   will

12b Exploring places

Vocabulary land and water

1 Complete the sentences about the places with these words.

| desert | forest | island | lake | mountain |
| ocean | river | sea | | |

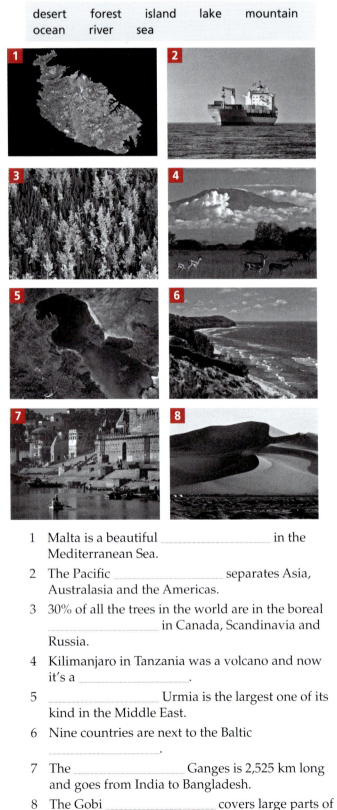

1 Malta is a beautiful _____ in the Mediterranean Sea.
2 The Pacific _____ separates Asia, Australasia and the Americas.
3 30% of all the trees in the world are in the boreal _____ in Canada, Scandinavia and Russia.
4 Kilimanjaro in Tanzania was a volcano and now it's a _____ .
5 _____ Urmia is the largest one of its kind in the Middle East.
6 Nine countries are next to the Baltic _____ .
7 The _____ Ganges is 2,525 km long and goes from India to Bangladesh.
8 The Gobi _____ covers large parts of southern Mongolia and northern China.

Grammar definite *the* or no article + names

2 Write *the* or Ø (no article) before these names of places.

1 _____ Maldive Islands
2 _____ Atlantic Ocean
3 _____ Europe
4 _____ Mount Kilimanjaro
5 _____ Malta
6 _____ River Nile
7 _____ Lake Balaton
8 _____ Peru
9 _____ Sahara Desert
10 _____ Asia
11 _____ River Mississippi
12 _____ Iceland
13 _____ Mediterranean Sea
14 _____ Black Forest
15 _____ Himalayan Mountains

3 There are three mistakes in this quiz. Cross out the extra word in three of the questions.

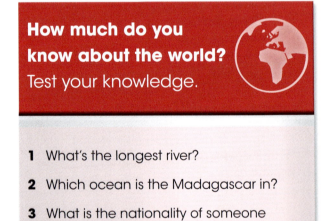

How much do you know about the world? Test your knowledge.

1 What's the longest river?
2 Which ocean is the Madagascar in?
3 What is the nationality of someone from the Netherlands?
4 Where is the Lake Vostok?
5 Which continent are the Alps in?
6 Where is the Mount Ararat?

4 Can you answer the questions in the quiz in Exercise 3? Check your answers on page 96.

Reading the highest place

5 Complete the article about Felix Baumgartner with these sentences (a–e).

a That's faster than the speed of sound.
b Felix Baumgartner is a skydiver.
c He jumped 31 kilometres in 1960.
d The balloon was 100 metres tall.
e 'Felix did a great job.'

Space jump

¹ _____ He is 43 years old and he has jumped from the tops of mountains and some of the tallest buildings in the world. On 24th October 2012 he jumped from the highest place above the Earth.

A balloon carried him to a height of 39 kilometres above the surface of the Earth. ² _____ From his special capsule, Baumgartner could see the Earth really well before he jumped back to Earth. The jump took him ten minutes. On the way down, he travelled at a speed of 1,342 kilometres an hour. ³ _____ He fell for four minutes twenty seconds before he opened his parachute.

Baumgartner now has the world record for jumping from the highest place above the Earth. Before Baumgartner, Joe Kittinger had the record. ⁴ _____ Kittinger is in his eighties now and he worked with Baumgartner. After the jump, Kittinger said: ⁵ _____

Word focus *how*

6 Complete the *how* questions with these words.

far   fast   high   long   old   tall   well

1 How _____ is Felix Baumgartner?
2 How _____ did the balloon carry him?
3 How _____ was the balloon?
4 How _____ could he see the Earth from his capsule?
5 How _____ did the jump take?
6 How _____ did he travel down to Earth?
7 How _____ did Joe Kittinger jump in 1960?

7 Read the article again. Then answer the questions from Exercise 6.

1 _____
2 _____
3 _____
4 _____
5 _____
6 _____
7 _____

Felix in his capsule above the Earth

12c Planets

Vocabulary the Earth and other planets

1 Complete the text about Pluto with these words.

> astronomers   orbit   planets   rock   star   surface   travel

The ¹_____ at the centre of our solar system is called the Sun. There are eight ²_____ in our solar system, including the Earth, and they all ³_____ the Sun. But before 2006, there were nine planets. Pluto was the smallest planet in our solar system. ⁴_____ discovered Pluto in 1930. Through a telescope, the ⁵_____ of Pluto looks different colours. It is made of ⁶_____ and ice. Humans could not live on Pluto so we will probably never ⁷_____ there. In 2006, scientists decided Pluto was not a planet.

Listening space news

2 🔊 2.38 Listen to a news programme. Match the numbers (1–4) with the information (a–d).

1 four _____
2 hundreds _____
3 six _____
4 thousands or millions _____

a the number of exoplanets that scientists have found since the nineties
b the number of exoplanets that scientists think are in the universe
c the number of light years between the region in space called Alpha Centauri and the Earth
d the number of exoplanets around a star two thousand light years away

3 Dictation the news

🔊 2.38 Listen again and complete the news report.

Here is the news. ¹_____ have found the nearest planet to our solar system. It ²_____ a star in the region of space called Alpha Centauri. That's four light years from the ³_____. The planet is similar in size to Earth, but it is very close to its star. For this reason, ⁴_____ could not live on it. However, stars often have more than one planet, so the ⁵_____ is exciting. It's possible that there are other planets in the same solar system.

Planets near other stars are called ⁶_____ and astronomers have found hundreds of them since the nineties. Using powerful telescopes, they look for a ⁷_____ in another solar system and then they look for planets orbiting it. Recently, astronomers found a star two thousand light years away with six ⁸_____ around it, and experts think there are probably thousands or millions more exoplanets in the ⁹_____.

Answers to 12b Exercise 4

1 the River Nile **2** the Indian Ocean **3** Dutch
4 Antarctica **5** Europe **6** Turkey

Unit 12 The Earth

12d A special day

Listening national tree planting day

1 🔊 **2.39** Listen to a presentation about a national tree planting day. Answer the questions.

1 Where is Joel from?

2 Which Friday in October is National Tree Planting Day?

3 How many trees have people planted across the island since 2002?

4 Who plants the trees?

5 Where do they plant them?

6 Where did Joel and the students plant new trees last year?

7 What does he hope other countries will do in the future?

Real life making a presentation

2 Match the stages of a presentation (1–7) with these sections of Joel's presentation (a–g).

1 Welcome the audience.
2 Introduce yourself.
3 Introduce the title of your presentation.
4 Talk about the history.
5 Talk about the present day.
6 Conclude the presentation.
7 End the presentation.

a First of all, National Tree Planting Day is on the first Friday of October every year. The first National Tree Planting Day was in 2002. Since then, people have planted fifty thousand trees across the island.
b Today, I'd like to talk about an important day in my country. It's called National Tree Planting Day.
c Good morning and thank you for coming.
d In conclusion, I really think National Tree Planting Day is important. In the future, I hope other countries will have the same day.
e Thank you very much for listening.
f Nowadays, everyone from schoolchildren to business people are involved in the day. They can get seeds from their local Forestry Department and they can plant the seeds in local parks and communities. Last year, I went with some students from my university and we planted new trees in the gardens of a home for old people.
g My name's Joel and I'm from Jamaica.

3 Pronunciation pausing on commas

🔊 **2.40** Listen to these sentences from a presentation. Listen for the pause and write in the missing comma.

1 Today I'd like to talk about an important day.
2 First of all my country's national day is on 4th July.
3 Since then people have always celebrated this day.
4 Nowadays everyone has a day off.
5 Next families have a big meal together.
6 In conclusion I really think it's important.

12e A tree planting poster

1 Writing skill important words and information

a Read these sentences for some posters. Delete the unnecessary words so you have the number of words in brackets.

1. Everyone ~~is~~ invited ~~to our~~ New Year's Party! (five words)
2. The Annual Party is at the Town Hall on 1st May. (eight words)
3. There is a huge sale at the Big Bed Shop all this week. (eight words)
4. You can eat delicious sandwiches at Jill's Café. (six words)
5. Visit the website www.greenfest.org for details. (four words)
6. The entrance to the disco is free. (four words)
7. Listen to live music and look at local art at the Mayberry Arts Festival. (nine words)
8. You are welcome to our Midsummer Party at nine. (six words)

b Read this information about National Tree Planting Day. Underline the most important words and information.

> You are invited to plant a tree on 7th October for National Tree Planting Day. We will give you free seeds to plant in the local park. There will be lots of people there and lots of entertainment, so bring the whole family. We'll have hot and cold food, and local shops will sell environmentally friendly products. We'll also have presentations about how to help the environment and information about gardening. The event is in Tenant Park, and it starts at two o'clock and it finishes at five o'clock. The entrance is five euros for adults and free for children under 16. You can telephone us on 088 678 4955 for more information.

Writing a poster

2 Write the important information from the text in Exercise 1b on this poster.

Wordbuilding word forms (2)

1 Label the diagram with these words.

height   depth   length   weight   width

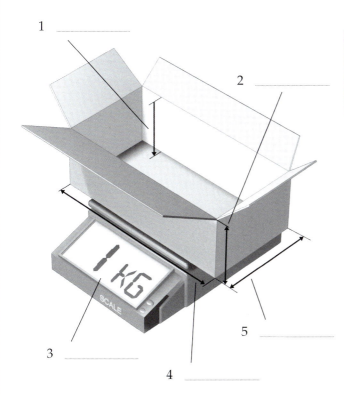

2 Complete the pairs of sentences with the correct form of the measurement words.

1 long / length
   a This film is very _____ .
   b What is the _____ of this film?
2 high / height
   a My son's _____ is about one metre.
   b How _____ is that mountain?
3 weigh / weight
   a The _____ is one kilogram.
   b These potatoes _____ one kilogram.
4 deep / depth
   a This swimming pool is very _____ .
   b Nobody knows the _____ of this lake.
5 wide / width
   a In some places, the Amazon River is 40 kilometres _____ .
   b The _____ of the Amazon River is bigger than any other river in the world.

3 Which measurement words in Exercise 2 are adjectives? Which word is a verb?

4 🔊 2.41 Listen and repeat the measurement words in Exercise 2.

Learning skills your learning

5 You are at the end of this course. Think about your learning using this questionnaire. Circle the number in Part 1 and answer the questions in Part 2. Then show the questionnaire to your teacher and discuss your answers.

Your learning

4 = Very good   3 = Good
2 = Satisfactory   1 = Not very good

1 How was your progress in …?

Vocabulary	4	3	2	1
Grammar	4	3	2	1
Useful phrases (in 'Real life')	4	3	2	1
Pronunciation	4	3	2	1
Reading	4	3	2	1
Listening	4	3	2	1
Speaking	4	3	2	1
Writing	4	3	2	1

2 What do you want to do in the future? Do you want to do another English course?

Give details:

Check!

6 What do these numbers refer to in Unit 12 of the Student's Book?

1 914 trillion litres

2 47 metres

3 2009

4 18 trillion

5 20 million

IELTS practice test

🔊 **2.42**

LISTENING TEST

SECTION 1 *Questions 1–10*

Questions 1 and 2

Choose the correct letter, A, B or C.

Example

Ian went to the library to find a book about
- (A) science.
- B sport.
- C history.

---

1 At the library, Ian saw
   - A an exhibition of photos.
   - B information about a lecture.
   - C a notice about a club to join.

2 Why is Ian going back to the library?
   - A to meet someone
   - B to collect something
   - C to take part in an activity

Questions 3–10

Complete the notes below.

Write **NO MORE THAN TWO WORDS AND/OR A NUMBER** *for each answer.*

Events at the Library

Day	Name of event	Time	Price per week
Monday	Photography club	7.30 p.m.	£2.50
3	Storytelling workshop	7.00 p.m.	4 ....
Thursday	5 .... club	2.00 p.m.	£1.50
6	Film club	7.45 p.m.	7 ....
Friday	Poetry workshop	8	£3.00
Saturday	9 .... design	10.15 a.m.	£4.75
Saturday	Map reading	2.45 p.m.	10 ....

SECTION 2

Questions 11–20

Questions 11–13

Choose the correct letter, **A**, **B** or **C**.

11 Which day is Hilary's interview?
    A Monday
    B Tuesday
    C Wednesday

12 Where should Hilary go first?
    A the main college reception
    B the personnel department
    C room number 341

13 Who will Hilary meet at the interview?
    A Wendy Bright
    B Howard Green
    C Diana Cook

Questions 14 and 15

Choose **TWO** letters, **A–F**.

What two things should Hilary take to her interview?

A a copy of the application form

B an identity document

C exam certificates

D a written reference

E her invitation letter

F a photo of herself

Questions 16–20

Complete the table below.

Write **NO MORE THAN TWO WORDS AND/OR A NUMBER** for each answer.

Job title:	Office assistant
Main duties:	• entering data • 16 .... • dealing with 17 ....
Number of hours per week:	18 ....
Basic rate of pay per hour:	19 ....
Paid annual holiday entitlement:	20 ....

SECTION 3

Questions 21–30

Questions 21 and 22

Choose the correct letter, A, B or C.

21 Which continent has the largest number of wild rabbits?
   A Europe
   B Australasia
   C North America

22 Wild rabbits usually live for
   A five to ten years.
   B ten to twelve years.
   C fifteen to eighteen years.

Questions 23–30

Complete the table below.

Write **NO MORE THAN TWO WORDS AND/OR A NUMBER** *for each answer.*

Keeping rabbits as pets: time and costs involved

Number of rabbits:	2
Total time needed per day:	**23** ....
Daily activities:	• give them food and water • **24** .... their living area • basic **25** .... check • giving them exercise
Cost of buying two rabbits:	£50
Microchipping:	**26** ....
Vaccinations (by vet):	£100
Accommodation:	rabbit house **27** ....
28 .... :	• water bowl £8.00 • food bowl **29** .... • other £20.00
Food:	£16.36 per week
Insurance:	£10.00 per **30** ....
Total cost of two rabbits for life:	£16,000 (10 years)

SECTION 4

Questions 31–40

Questions 31–34

Choose the correct letter, A, B or C.

31 What should the students do each week?
   A Run a fixed distance.
   B Run at a constant speed.
   C Run for a certain period of time.

32 What does the speaker say about jogging?
   A It's best to go with a partner.
   B You should always try to feel relaxed.
   C Don't try to talk and jog at the same time.

33 Students who already do other sports
   A can continue with them during the training.
   B need to ask the trainer for advice.
   C may not have to train so much.

34 Where should students do the training?
   A on a sports track
   B on the grass in a park
   C on roads and pavements

Questions 35–40

Complete the notes below.

*Write **NO MORE THAN TWO WORDS** for each answer.*

TRAINING PROGRAMME

Length of the programme: 35 ....

What to wear:
 • the type of shorts that 36 .... usually wear
 • 37 .... specially designed for runners

What not to wear: clothes made from 38 ....

If you start to feel hungry, you should 39 .... something.

Stop training if you have caught a 40 ....

READING TEST

SECTION 1

Questions 1–10

Questions 1–10
*Look at the six advertisements for part-time jobs, **A–F**.*
For which jobs are the following statements true?
*Write the correct letter (**A–F**) in boxes 1–10 on your answer sheet.*
***NB** You may use letters more than once.*

1 You only get one free day per week in this job.
2 This job offers the highest rate of pay.
3 You get free transport to work in this job.
4 You can eat for nothing at work.
5 You have to wear special clothes at work.
6 You have to take money from customers in this job.
7 Language skills are useful in this job.
8 This job only lasts for a limited period.
9 There may be more work available in the future.
10 You have to work closely with other people in this job.

A

Supermarket cashier

Monday to Friday evenings only

No previous experience necessary

£5.30 per hour

10% discount in store (food items only)

Clean and tidy appearance essential

B

Hamburger Chef

Weekend lunchtimes and evenings

Cooking experience an advantage

£5.25 per hour

Free meals when on duty

Uniform provided

C

Coffee bar staff

07.00–09.30 six days a week

To work espresso machine only

Very busy bar – you have to work in a team

£5.50 per hour

Ability to speak French or Spanish an advantage

D

Hotel Receptionist

Weekend lunchtimes only

11.30–15.30

£4.50 per hour

Possibility of extra hours next month

Close to the railway station

E

Suburban Hospital Canteen Porter

- Afternoons: Tuesday to Saturday 16.00–18.00
- £4.75 per hour
- No cooking skills needed
- To take meals to patients
- Weekly bus ticket to the city centre provided

F

Hotel chambermaid

Three mornings a week

08.00–11.00

Temporary contract (six weeks)

£4.50 per hour

City-centre location

SECTION 2

Questions 11–20

Questions 11–20

Read the text on page 107.

Do the following statements agree with the information given in the text?

In boxes 11–20 on your answer sheet, write

> *TRUE*   *if the statement agrees with the information*
> *FALSE*   *if the statement contradicts the information*
> *NOT GIVEN*   *if there is no information on this*

11 The survey was part of the students' course.

12 The people who answered the students' questions all live in the same city.

13 The students sometimes asked different questions.

14 The students were surprised at how difficult the survey was to do.

15 Most people said that walking was their favourite activity.

16 Swimming is more popular than keep-fit exercises.

17 Most people who like walking prefer to do it in the countryside.

18 Walking holidays are more popular than other types of activity holiday.

19 More men than women go on walking holidays.

20 Boating holidays and golfing holidays are equally popular with unmarried people.

Leisure Survey

Recently, students at the city's university carried out a survey about free-time activities and holidays as part of their course. They wanted to find out if city residents like to be active in their free time. They also wanted to find out which sporting activities are the most popular and if different types of people prefer different activities.

The students asked a sample of local inhabitants to take part in the survey and asked them all the same questions. The students were quite surprised by some of the things they found. But if you compare their findings with national statistics, the people taking part in the survey are not unusual.

The first question the students asked people was about their favourite sporting activity. About 12% of the people they asked said that the leisure activity they enjoyed doing most in their free time was walking. This was the most popular activity. In second place in the list was swimming. Nine per cent of the people said that they liked doing that best, and in third place came keep-fit exercises.

The next questions the students asked were about how often people did their favourite activity and how long they spent on it. They discovered, for example, that people who like walking spend 108 minutes each month on average on their hobby. These people walk for an average of about five miles per month. But some walkers do less than that. For instance, a lot of people just go for a walk round their local park after lunch at the weekend. And, of course, some walkers do a lot more. For example, the statistic includes a few very keen walkers who go for long walks in the countryside most weekends.

The students asked the people in their survey about holidays too. Activity holidays, where people go on a holiday to do a sporting activity, are very popular in Britain, and walking holidays are the most popular of all. The students found that this was just as true of local people as it is nationally.

But what type of people take these holidays? The students found out that most people who go on walking holidays are under 35 years of age. The majority of these people have jobs, and more than 50% of them are single. There were an equal number of men and women going on walking holidays, and the same is true of cycling holidays. Golfing holidays, however, were different. Eighty per cent of people who said they went on golfing holidays were male. Boating holidays, on the other hand, are the ones where you find the largest number of single people.

Not everybody likes activity holidays, however. Sixty-two per cent of the people in the survey have not been on this type of holiday in the last five years. However, 12% of these people said they would like to go on one in the future.

SECTION 3

Questions 21–29

Read the text on page 109 and answer questions 21–29.

Questions 21–27

The text on page 109 has seven sections, **A–G**.

Choose the correct heading for sections **A–G** from the list of headings below.

Write the correct number (**i–ix**) in boxes **21–27** on your answer sheet.

> **List of Headings**
> i   How fit must I be?
> ii What about overnight accommodation?
> iii Are these holidays expensive?
> iv What must I take with me when I'm cycling?
> v   How far can I cycle on this type of holiday?
> vi Are these holidays good for all ages?
> vii What can go wrong on cycling holidays?
> viii Are cycling holidays good for the environment?
> ix Who organises cycling holidays?

21 Section A
22 Section B
23 Section C
24 Section D
25 Section E
26 Section F
27 Section G

Questions 28 and 29

Complete the sentences below.

Choose **NO MORE THAN TWO WORDS** from the text for each answer.

The writer gives the example of **28** .... as a place where cycling may be more difficult.

The writer uses the term **29** .... holiday to describe a type of cycling holiday where you sleep in the same place each night.

Eco Escapes: Cycling Holidays

Section A

Are you worried about the amount of pollution you cause when you go away on holiday? Both public transport and cars can cause real damage to places that lots of tourists visit, and some people think that this is wrong. Many British people fly to seaside resorts in places like Spain and Greece on what are called 'package holidays', which can leave quite a big carbon footprint. That's why more and more people are choosing a different type of holiday. Cycling holidays are much greener than holidays by car, train or plane – and you get lots of good exercise as well. So, as well as having a break and seeing different places, you can keep fit too.

Section B

There are different ways of going on a cycling holiday. Of course, there is nothing to stop you going on your own if you want, but often groups of people travel together and plan a route in advance, which may be more fun. Or you may prefer to book a holiday that has been put together by a company which makes all the arrangements in advance, so that you have no worries. On this type of holiday, you also have the chance to make friends with other people who are on the same trip.

Section C

And there are different types of cycling holiday on offer. Serious cyclists sometimes want to travel a long distance every day, because for them the joy of cycling at speed is part of the fun of the holiday. Other people are more interested in seeing the scenery and exploring the places they pass through, and so they are happy to travel more slowly. It's up to you what distance you want to cover every day, and most holiday companies offer a range of possibilities to suit the needs of different types of people.

Section D

Many people who go on cycling holidays use a bicycle regularly and choose this type of holiday because they know that they enjoy cycling. So what about if you have never cycled, or if you haven't been on a bike since you were a young child? It's a good idea to do some training before your holiday, especially if you are new to cycling or out of practice. It isn't necessary to be very strong to ride a bike, but you should be in good health. Cycling in Scotland, for instance, where there are lots of hills, will give you a good physical workout. But if that sounds too much like hard work, choose an area like East Anglia where the landscape is mostly flat.

Section E

There are also a range of options when it comes to how long to stay away and how to make sure you have a bed for the night. Some people prefer what's known as a 'centre-based' holiday, for example, where you return to the same hotel every evening and can have a good meal and a shower. Other people prefer to follow a continuous route – so that they sleep in a different place each night, sometimes carrying a tent with them so that they can go camping.

Section F

Clearly, it is not practical to cycle with lots of luggage. Holiday companies sometimes arrange for your suitcases to be sent on to your next destination, so that they are there waiting for you when you arrive in the evening. This means that you only need to carry a few things with you every day. Some different types of clothing are a good idea in case the weather changes suddenly, and a good map and an emergency repair kit for your bike are essential.

Section G

How much your holiday costs will depend on which type you choose. If you want to explore another country or another continent, like Africa or Australia, then you have to travel there before you can start cycling, and that can be expensive. However, camping can be a way of keeping accommodation costs down. But, generally speaking, you will find there is a cycling holiday to suit every pocket.

SECTION 4

Questions 30–40

Read the text on page 111 and answer questions 30–40.

Questions 30 and 31

Complete the sentences below.

Choose **NO MORE THAN TWO WORDS** from the text for each answer.

Cuckoos usually arrive in Europe in the month of **30** ....

Adult cuckoos usually leave Europe in the month of **31** ....

Questions 32–40

For each question 32–40 decide which answer is correct.

Write one letter, **A**, **B** or **C**, next to questions 32–40.

> **A** only the bird called Lyster
> **B** the birds called Chris and Lyster
> **C** all five birds

Which bird or birds:

32 was (or were) born in England?
33 reached the Congo?
34 flew over Morocco?
35 returned to Norfolk?
36 left England with a satellite tag?
37 successfully crossed the Sahara twice?
38 travelled at least 10,000 miles with a tag?
39 flew over Algeria?
40 only flew over Spain once?

Backpacking cuckoos

The cuckoo is a bird which people all over Europe know from the sound it makes. It doesn't sing, but makes a noise with one high note and one low note – 'coo coo'. People in Europe say that when you hear that sound for the first time each year, you know that spring has arrived. In some years, people hear cuckoos as early as February, and in other years they don't arrive until April. But March is the typical month for the birds to arrive. This is because the cuckoo lives in Africa during the winter months and only comes to Europe when the weather gets better.

People have always known that the cuckoos migrated. They fly thousands of miles across the Sahara desert twice a year – once in the spring and then back again at the end of the summer, normally in July. The young cuckoos are born in England and they leave for Africa a little later. But by mid-August, there are no cuckoos left in Europe. The details of how they make their incredible journey have only recently been understood by scientists.

Last May, scientists caught five male birds in Norfolk in eastern England. They put a tiny satellite tag on each bird's back, and then set them free again. The tag allowed the scientists to see where there went when they left England.

The scientists found that the five tagged birds all travelled about 10,000 miles that summer, and all spent the winter in the Congo region of central Africa. Incredibly, the scientists discovered that the five birds all took different routes to reach their destination in Africa. The first bird, to which the scientists gave the name Lyster, flew across France, Spain and Morocco before crossing the Sahara desert. The second bird, called Chris, went by a completely different route. He flew over Belgium, Germany and Italy before crossing the Sahara desert in Libya. Tunisia and Algeria were countries that the other three birds flew over on their way to Africa.

The scientists were also able to see that all five birds left Africa again, nine months later, to come back to Britain. Incredibly, they each took a different route again. And not only a different route from each other, but a different route from the one they had taken before. For example, Lyster flew back to England via Algeria and France, but this time didn't fly over Spain and Morocco. Chris also crossed the Algerian desert, but then continued his journey via Italy and France. The two birds, however, both returned to the exact place in Norfolk where their satellite tags were fitted the year before. The three other birds did not return to England and the scientists think they died on their return journey.

Next year, the scientists are going to put satellite tags on female birds to see which route they take.

WRITING TEST

TASK 1

You should spend about 20 minutes on this task.

> You recently had lunch in an expensive restaurant, but you didn't like the food. When you told the waiter, he was rude to you.
>
> Write a letter to the manager of the restaurant. In your letter:
> - tell the manager why you didn't like the food
> - explain what happened when you told the waiter
> - say what you would like the manager to do.

Write at least 150 words.

You do not need to write any addresses.

Begin your letter like this:

Dear Sir or Madam,

TASK 2

You should spend about 40 minutes on this task.

Write about this topic.

> Some people think it is good to listen to music while they are studying.
>
> Do you agree or disagree?

Give reasons for your answer and include any relevant examples from your own knowledge or experience.

Write at least 250 words.

SPEAKING TEST

PART 1

Let's talk about your family.
- How many people are there in your family?
- What jobs do the people in your family do?
- Do other people in your family speak English?
- What do you do with your family on special occasions?

PART 2

Candidate Task Card

> Describe a typical day in your life.
>
> You should say:
> - the things you do every day
> - what time you do these things
> - the things you like and the things you don't like doing
> - explain who you meet during the day.

You will have to talk about the topic for one or two minutes.

You will have one minute to think about what you are going to say.

You can make some notes to help you if you wish.

Rounding-off questions
- Which is your favourite part of the day? Why?
- What do you like doing at the weekend?

PART 3

First of all, let's talk about sport in general.
- Which sports do you like? Why?
- Which sports are better to watch and which sports are better to play?
- Do you think everybody should play sport? Why / Why not?

Finally, let's talk about famous sportspeople.
- Do you think that some sportspeople earn too much money? Why / Why not?

Audioscripts

Unit 1

1.1
N = Narrator, I = Interviewer, T = Tierney Thys
N: This month we interviewed two new explorers. Our interviewer, Michelle Bright, telephoned them in the Galapagos Islands and Canada.
T: My name is Tierney Thys.
I: Where are you from?
T: I'm from the state of California, but I'm not there at the moment.
I: Where are you now?
T: I'm in the Galapagos Islands.
I: What's your job?
T: I'm a scientist.
I: Is your husband a scientist?
T: No, he isn't. He's an engineer.

JT = Josh Thome, I = Interviewer
JT: My name's Josh Thome.
I: Who is the other person in the photo?
JT: He's Sol. We work together.
I: Are you from the USA?
JT: No, we aren't. We're from Canada.
I: Are you the same age?
JT: No, we aren't. I'm thirty-six and Sol is thirty-five.
I: Are your jobs the same?
JT: Yes, they are. We're film-makers.

1.2
I = Interviewer, J = Jon
I: What's your name?
J: My name's Jon Aanenson.
I: Are you from Norway?
J: Yes, I'm from the city of Bergen, but I'm not there at the moment.
I: Where are you?
J: I'm in Greenland.
I: What is your job?
J: I'm a scientist.
I: Is your wife a scientist?
J: No, she isn't. She's a writer.

1.3
A = Ati, I = Interviewer
A: Hello, my name's Ati. I'm an archaeologist.
I: Where are you from?
A: Egypt.
I: Are you there at the moment?
A: Yes, I'm here with my husband.
I: Is he an archaeologist?
A: Yes, he is, but he isn't from Egypt. He's from England.
I: Are you the same age?
A: No, we aren't. I'm thirty-five and he's thirty-eight.

1.4
1 What's your name?
2 Are you from England?
3 How old are you?
4 Are you married or single?
5 Are you a student?
6 What is your address?

1.6
There are big forests between the Republic of the Congo and the Central African Republic. Thousands of gorillas are in the region. They live in groups and large families. Kingo is the head of one family in the region. He's a Silverback Gorilla and he's huge! He's 30 years old and he's the father.

Kingo's wives are Mama, Mekome, Beatrice and Ugly. Mekome is Kingo's favourite wife but Mama is the most important adult female gorilla. There are also four young gorillas, two boys and two girls. Mama's son is Kusu. Mekome's son is Ekendy. Beatrice and Ugly are the girls' mothers. Their daughters are Gentil and Bomo.

The family is together all the time and they travel two kilometres a day. Kusu, Ekendy, Gentil and Bomo watch their father and mothers and they learn to find the fruit on different trees. After lunch, the children play with Kingo.

1.8
1 a They're in London.
  b Their family is in London.
2 a He's my brother.
  b His brother is a scientist.
3 a Are you from Canada?
  b Our family is from Canada.
4 a You're eighteen.
  b Your sister is eighteen.

1.9
Malaysia is in south-east Asia. There are two parts to the country with the South China Sea between them. There are 28 million people in the country and 1.6 million live in the capital city of Kuala Lumpur. The average age of the country is 27 years. There are a lot of different religions in the country and 60% of the population are Muslim. The main language of the country is Malay but a lot of people also speak English. Malaysia has modern cities and beautiful countryside. Over 60% of the population use the Internet.

1.13
C = Conference manager, Z = Dr Zull, P = Beata Polit
C: Hello, can I help you?
Z: Yes, I'm here for the conference.
C: What's your name?
Z: Doctor Zull. I'm from Australia.
C: Zull. Zull. Zull. Is that Z-U-L-L?
Z: That's right.
C: Oh, here you are. Zull. Nice to meet you, Doctor Zull. My name's Stella Williams. I'm the conference manager.
Z: Nice to meet you too.
C: So, here is some information about the conference. You're early so you can have a coffee over there. In fact, let me introduce you to someone. Beata?
P: Hello?
C: Beata, I'd like to introduce you to Doctor Zull. He's also at the conference.
P: Nice to meet you. My name's Beata Polit.
Z: Nice to meet you too, Beata. How do you spell your surname?
P: P-O-L-I-T
Z: So where are you from?
P: Poland. And you?
Z: Australia.
C: So, let me leave you both.
Z: OK. Thanks, Stella. Nice talking to you.
C: Yes. See you later.
Z&P: Goodbye.

Unit 2

1.14
I = Interviewer, C = Climber
I: Is this your rucksack?
C: Yes, it is. And these are maps for my next climb.
I: Is this a first-aid kit?
C: Yes, it's very important. And also this torch. In fact, there are two torches in my rucksack, and a compass.
I: Where is your next climb?
C: In the Himalayas. It's cold there and these are my gloves. And this is a good hat.
I: Are these your boots?
C: Yes, they are.

1.16
About nineteen million passengers use Stockholm-Arlanda airport every year. Aeroplanes take off and land all the time, but at the side of the runway there's a big Boeing 747 aeroplane and it never takes off. That's because it's a hostel called 'Jumbo Stay'. It's only fifteen minutes on foot from the main airport terminal or five minutes by bus.

The Jumbo Stay is a real aeroplane from 1976 and from the outside you think it's a normal aeroplane. But on the inside it's very different. There's a reception desk and a twenty-four-hour-a-day café in the old first-class seating area.

There aren't any aeroplane seats. There are twenty-seven rooms with seventy-six beds. Each room has one or two beds, a TV and the Internet. The rooms are small but cheap, and visitors usually only stay for a night. You can also sleep in the cockpit of the aeroplane. It's more expensive but it's a private double room with a shower. Jumbo Stay is very popular with families and with travellers who want a different kind of travel experience.

1.17
IKEA is a global company with IKEA shops all over the world. There are 300 IKEA shops in 36 different countries. Over five million people shop at IKEA every year.

The company is famous for furniture and products for the home. You can buy beds, chairs, sofas, kitchen cupboards and office desks. It sells more than 10,000 different items.

IKEA furniture is often made in Sweden but company products are from 50 different countries. For example, one factory in Poland makes 30 million tables, desks and wardrobes a year.

IKEA also has other services. There are restaurants in the shops and the food is Swedish. There is an IKEA mobile phone service in the United Kingdom. And in some countries you can even buy a house from IKEA.

1.19
A: Shop assistant, C = Customer
Conversation 1
A: Hello, can I help you?
C: Yes, I'd like a hat, please.
A: Which size?
C: I don't know. What size is this one?
A: That's the small one.
C: Yes, it is very small. What about this one?
A: That's the large one.
C: It's perfect. How much is it?
A: Fifteen pounds.

Conversation 2
A: Hello, can I help you?
C: Yes, I'd like a bag, please.
A: Which one?
C: Are they all the same?
A: No, this one is ten dollars and this one is ten dollars fifty.
C: And that one?
A: Ten dollars ninety-nine.
C: OK. Give me that one, please.
A: This one for ten dollars?
C: Yes please.

Conversation 3
A: Hello, can I help you?
C: Yes, I'd like a coffee, please.
A: Sure. Milk and sugar?
C: Err, just milk, please. No sugar.

🔊 **1.20**

Conversation 1
A: Hello, can I help you?
A: Which size?

Conversation 2
A: Hello, can I help you?
A: Which one?

Conversation 3
A: Hello, can I help you?
A: Milk and sugar?

Unit 3

🔊 **1.22**

1
Would passengers for flight BA3455 please go to Gate 13. The flight for Dublin is ready for boarding. That's passengers for flight BA3455.
A: Quick, it's quarter past two. Let's go to the gate.

2
M = Martin, V = Vera
M: Hello?
V: Hi Martin. It's Vera!
M: Oh, hi Vera.
V: How are you?
M: Err, OK. Actually a bit tired. It's the middle of the night. How's your trip round Australia?
V: Oh no! I'm sorry. It's half past two in the afternoon here.
M: That's OK.
V: Sorry. Go back to sleep. I'll call you in the morning – your morning, my evening.

3
The time is twelve o'clock. And here is the news. It's the first of January and thousands of people across the world celebrated New Year's Day. Here in London, thousands of people walked through the streets and watched fireworks across the city.

4
A: Excuse me. What time does the next train to Stuttgart leave?
B: One moment. Let me look. There's one at twenty-five past ten.
A: But it's twenty-five to eleven.
B: Oh, yes. You're too late for that one. OK, the next one is in ten minutes from Platform 6.
A: Thanks.

🔊 **1.23**
1 What do you do?
2 Where do you live?
3 Do you go to work by car?
4 What time do you eat lunch?
5 Do you like shopping?

🔊 **1.24**

1 I don't have a normal day because I work all over the world. I have a studio, but a lot of my photos are of animals in different places.

2 I work in the centre of the city in a hospital. I start at nine every morning and sometimes I work until nine at night.

3 I have two jobs. One is in a small café at lunchtimes and then I also work in an expensive restaurant in the centre of Paris at night.

4 We can go away for about three months and so I'm often not at home. In fact, I spend more time on the boat than in my house.

5 I work for a large firm in an office building. We work with a lot of different companies.

6 My classes are three days a week so I go to the university on Mondays, Wednesdays and Thursdays. The rest of the week I study at home or meet friends in the city.

7 I arrive at the airport early because I fly from London to New York. It's about eight hours there and eight hours back.

8 I don't work in a normal classroom. I have an office and I teach my students through my computer and the Internet.

🔊 **1.26**

Part 1
On this chart there are three important percentages. The first, 7%, shows the number of native speakers in the world. So, for example, in countries like the USA, Australia, Ireland and the United Kingdom. The next percentage is for non-native speakers, and that's 15%. These people learn English and use it every day in their work or for their studies. And the rest of the world doesn't speak English. That's 78%.

Part 2
For a long time, the only language on the Internet was English. But nowadays there are lots of different languages and here are the top five. So, English is still number one with around 540 million users. But Chinese is also popular with 450 million users. Then Spanish, Japanese and Portuguese with 160, 100 and 85 million users.

Part 3
There are around 7,000 languages in the world and this chart shows them by region. Asia and Africa have the most different languages. Then countries in the Pacific region have 19% and The Americas have 15%. And look at Europe with only 3% of the world's languages. Of course, the number is small but the languages are some of the big languages like English and Spanish …

1.27
1 There are 30 students in my class.
2 We're in New York on the 15th of May.
3 The price is 66 pounds.
4 I was third in the marathon.
5 My grandfather is 80 this year.

1.29
T = Tourist, L = Local person

1
T: Excuse me. I need a bank. Is there one near here?
L: Yes, it's near. Go straight up this street and take the first street on the right. Then turn left and it's there.

2
T: Hello. Where is the theatre? The play starts in ten minutes.
L: That's OK. It's about two minutes away. Go across this road and go past a car park on your right. Then take the first street on the left. It's on the corner.

3
T: Hello. Is the tourist information centre near here?
L: Err, it's about ten minutes away. Go straight up this street and turn left at the end. Go across a small park and the information centre is on the other side of it.

Unit 4

1.30
I = Interviewer, C = Customer
I: Hello, I work for the sports centre and we'd like to know more about our customers. Can I ask you some questions about your free time?
C: Sure.
I: Great. OK. So, first of all, do you play team sports at the sports centre?
C: Well, I play tennis. But that isn't a team sport. Err, so the answer is no.
I: OK. And what about martial arts? You know, like Tae Kwon Do or Judo?
C: Yes, I do Judo on Tuesday evenings. I really like it. It's fun.
I: OK. That's good. And do you go to the gym?
C: Yes. That's the main reason I come here. It's really good for me.
I: I see. And on our website we have training videos. Do you ever watch them?
C: No, I don't. What are they?
I: We made some videos about exercise and how you can do more exercise at home as well as in the gym. They're really useful.
C: Right. Sounds interesting.
I: And my last question. Do you meet friends in the café?
C: Yes, sometimes. I go to the gym with friends and sometimes we have a coffee in the café afterwards. It's relaxing.
I: So the answer is yes. OK. Thanks. That's everything.

1.32
F = Friend, MA = Model answer
1 F: Do you like swimming?
   MA: Yes, I do. It's relaxing and it's good for me.
2 F: What kind of music do you like?
   MA: I like listening to rock music.
3 F: Do you like playing computer games?
   MA: No, I don't.
4 F: What's your favourite sport?
   MA: I like watching and playing football.
5 F: Why do you like it?
   MA: It's exciting.

1.33
a John often travels abroad.
b Shannon and Nicole are always busy.
c He doesn't often have time.
d How often does Shannon surf?
e I read a newspaper every morning.
f Michael is often tired.

1.34
I = Interviewer, C = Claude Geraldo
I: Welcome to Extreme Sports Special and in today's programme we're talking to Claude Geraldo, a base jumper. Claude, first of all, tell us what base jumping is.
C: It's parachuting, but you don't do it from an aeroplane or a moving object. You jump from a fixed place like a tall building or the top of a cliff or mountain. And then you open your parachute before you hit the ground.
I: And why do you like it?
C: Well, I like physical sports like rugby and football, and at weekends I often go rock climbing with friends. But base jumping is amazing. I like it because it's so exciting.
I: So where do you learn to base jump?
C: You need to learn to parachute. So I learned from an aeroplane before I started on mountains.
I: But aren't you scared?
C: Sure. Every time I stand at the top of a cliff or a mountain, I'm a bit scared, but I think that's important. I like the adrenaline, but I always concentrate more because base jumping is a dangerous sport. Not everyone can do it.
I: Why do you say that?
C: Well, you need to be very fit and very strong. I mean physically strong, but also mentally strong.
I: OK. So the important piece of equipment is the parachute.
C: Right. I always check my parachute carefully before I put it on my back.
I: And is base jumping more dangerous than jumping from an aeroplane?
C: Yes, it is. Much more dangerous. It isn't as high as an aeroplane, but when you jump from a mountain, you can hit the side of the mountain. In fact, it's probably the most dangerous of all the extreme sports.
I: I see. Goodness me!

🔘 **1.35**
I = Interviewer, H = Hailey
I: So Hailey, you're here for the job of children's summer school helper.
H: Yes, that's right.
I: I want to ask you a few questions and at the end you can ask me some questions too. Let me check some information on your application form. You're 21. Is that correct?
H: Actually, I'm 22. My birthday was yesterday.
I: Oh, OK. 22. And you have dual nationality?
H: That's right. My father is Irish and my mother is Italian.
I: So, how well can you speak Italian?
H: Yes, I was born there so I'm fluent.
I: On the summer school we teach French to the children. Can you speak French?
H: Yes, I can a bit. It's elementary.
I: That's OK. We teach the children simple words and songs in French.
H: That's fine. I can do that.
I: We also do sports with the children. Are you good at playing tennis or football?
H: I can play tennis a bit, and I'm not bad at basketball.
I: Good. And we also have activities with art and music. Do you like art or can you play a musical instrument?
H: I'm not very good at painting or art but I like playing the guitar.
I: That sounds great. When can you start? We need someone from the twentieth.
H: Oh sorry, I can't start before the twenty-seventh.
I: Well, that might be OK …

Unit 5

🔘 **1.38**
1 Do you eat a lot of fruit and vegetables?
2 Do you eat a lot of meat, cheese and bread?
3 Do you eat a lot of desserts?
4 Do you eat much salad?
5 Do you do many sports?
6 Do you do many free-time activities like dancing or gardening?
7 Do you drink a lot of water?
8 Do you buy much fresh food?

🔘 **1.39**
1
A: Hello. Do you want something to drink?
B: Yes, I'd like some sparkling water, please.
A: A glass or a bottle?
B: A glass, please.

2
A: Hello, I'd like some rice for a curry, please.
B: How much?
A: A kilo, please.

3
A: I need some sauce for lamb. It's for a barbecue.
B: This one is nice.
A: Is it hot?
B: Very.
A: OK. I'll take a bottle of that one, please.

4
A: That looks nice.
B: It is. It's chocolate from Switzerland. Would you like a piece?
A: Thanks.

5
A: That was a good breakfast.
B: Are you still hungry?
A: No thanks, but that bread is good.
B: Have another slice.
A: Err, OK. Just a slice.

6
A: We need something for lunch in the park.
B: I've got some bread so we can make sandwiches.
A: But we haven't got anything to go in the sandwiches.
B: How about this tin of tuna?
A: Yes, that'll be OK.

🔘 **1.40**
Part 1
Nowadays, humans regularly travel into space and we often see astronauts on TV. It's easy to forget how amazing space travel is. Scientists spend years working on new technology and they find ways to make life in space possible. One basic problem is space food because it's difficult to transport into space. It's also difficult to eat food in space because there's no gravity. Space food and drink can float around in space. For example, a piece of bread flies through the air or coffee doesn't stay in a cup.

Part 2
The menu on a modern space ship is similar to food on Earth. Astronauts can eat beef, chicken, eggs and chocolate. But it all comes out of packets and they drink tea or coffee through a straw. Astronauts with NASA can choose their food. They visit the Space Food Systems Laboratory in Texas a few months before their flight. They taste, smell and eat different food and choose their favourites for the journey. In space, astronauts eat three meals a day and need 2,000 calories per day.

Part 3
Nowadays, astronauts stay in space longer and longer so the problem of food is more and more difficult. At the International Space Station, they make more water by recycling water from the air inside the space station. But in the future, scientists plan to grow and make food in space, so that astronauts can live there for years.

1.42
W = Waiter, C = Customer
W: Here's your table. And here is the menu. Can I get you anything to drink first?
C: Yes, I'd like some water, please.
W: Sparkling or still?
C: Still, please. Actually, I'll have sparkling. A bottle.
W: OK.
W: Here you are. And are you ready to order?
C: Yes, I'll have tomato soup and then the chicken kabsa sounds interesting.
W: Yes, it's a Middle Eastern dish.
C: Great.
W: And would you like a small salad with that?
C: Err, yes. I'll have a small green salad.

W: Finished?
C: Yes, thanks. That was delicious.
W: Any dessert?
C: Err, no, I don't want a dessert, but I'd like a cup of coffee.
W: Sure.
C: And could I have the bill, please?

1.44
You can buy pasta in a shop, but you can also make pasta and it tastes better. You need the following food: an egg, some flour and olive oil. Put the flour in a bowl and mix the egg and olive oil. Knead the mixture and make a ball of dough. Next, you need a pasta machine. Put the pasta dough through the machine until it is very flat. Then, cut the pasta into long, thin strips with a knife.

Unit 6

1.46
1 You'll never believe this. I bought a lottery ticket at a shop yesterday. I never do that normally! But I saw the lottery ticket and thought, why not? Anyway, I watched TV last night and my six numbers were on the screen! I definitely won some money, but I don't know how much yet.

2 I had a very busy week at work. I worked fourteen hours every day. It means I earn a lot of overtime pay but I don't want to do it every week. Anyway, it's the weekend now and I can relax.

3 Is there anything else on TV? This programme is all about banking and why it's important to save money. I know it's important, but I'm really not interested.

4 My friend has this new business. He buys things on the Internet and sells them again. He buys everything: books, clothes, electronics. Anyway, he wants me to work with him. I'm not sure but maybe it's a good way to make some extra money.

1.48
In 2001 I lived in France. I studied French at university. After university I wanted to live in France so I returned in 2003. I worked in a currency exchange office in Paris. I liked the job and I travelled all over the country at weekends. Last year I started a job in a bank and I married a Frenchwoman.

1.49
I'm in the middle of Kenya. The nearest town is twenty miles away but there's a garage on the road. I've stopped my car and I want some petrol. The person in the garage doesn't need my money. Instead, I have my mobile phone. We click a few keys on the phone and I pay. No cash, no waiting.

In many countries, paying by mobile phone is new technology, but in Kenya the method is more and more normal. The service is called M-Pesa and began in 2007. By 2010, over 50% of the population used this method of payment. And it isn't just in big cities. You can see farmers in small villages with their mobile phones, buying and selling their food and animals.

So how does M-Pesa work? Well, customers go into a shop with the M-Pesa logo. They pay cash and the shop puts credit on their phone. Then they can pay for something with a mobile phone by sending a text. The person who receives the text goes to another M-Pesa shop and shows the text message. Then the M-Pesa shop gives the person the money.

Now, around fifteen million people use M-Pesa in Kenya. Because it's so successful, other countries are starting to use M-Pesa or similar ways of paying. It's another example of how mobile technology changes our lives in a positive way, and how close we are to a world without cash.

1.50
1
A: Hello. I'm with a local charity. We collect money for a local hospital. We want to buy some new medical equipment for the children's part of the hospital. Could you give us some money today?
B: Err, I'm afraid I don't have any money.
A: Oh dear. Well, there's a bank around the corner so you could get some money.

2
A: Hello, can I ask you something?
B: Yes, of course. What's the problem?
A: Well, I want to transfer money online from one bank account to another. But I can't open my account.
B: You need a password.
A: Oh! Do I?

3
A: Sorry, but I don't have any money until the end of the month. Could you lend me some?
B: How much?
A: Two hundred?
B: Two hundred! I'm sorry, but I can't.
A: Well, what about one hundred?

4
A: Hi. Can I borrow some money?
B: How much?
A: Just a pound. I want a cup of coffee from the machine.
B: Yes, certainly. Here you are.

1.53
F = Friend, MA = Model answer
1 F: Can you help me?
  MA: Yes, certainly.
2 F: Can I borrow some money?
  MA: I'm afraid I don't have any money.
3 F: Could you lend me some money?
  MA: I'm sorry but I can't.
4 F: Can I ask you something?
  MA: Yes, of course.

Unit 7

2.1
Albatross: This is the albatross. In the life of a 50-year-old albatross, it flies six million kilometres. That's because of its wings. The wings of an albatross are longer than any other bird on Earth. An adult albatross has wings of 3.5 metres and a parent albatross can fly further than 15,000 kilometres to feed a chick.

Zebra: In the middle of Africa, there are 200,000 zebras. These beautiful animals are famous for their black and white coats, but their lives are more dangerous and difficult because of their long journey. Every year they go on a migration of a thousand kilometres across Africa.

Elephant seal: The ocean around Antarctica is colder than other parts of the world, but for elephant seals it is their home. These elephant seals go on journeys of 13,000 kilometres and can dive 1,500 metres. That's deeper than a human submarine. They can stay under the water for longer than two hours and only come up for air for a few minutes.

2.3
Seamounts are mountains that you cannot see above the sea. There are about 100,000 in the Earth's oceans which are over a kilometre high, but we don't know much about them. That's because the journey to a lot of these seamounts is long and difficult.

Las Gemelas is an area of seamounts about 500 kilometres from the coast of Costa Rica. The highest part of Las Gemelas is 2,286 metres and it's interesting for scientists because of the sea life on the sides of the mountains.

Avi Klapfer, Gregory Stone and Brian Skerry took a submersible called the DeepSee to Las Gemelas. It's a small submersible, but it has a lot of scientific equipment. As the DeepSee takes the three men towards Las Gemelas, they can see fish and coral. The higher part of the seamounts is the most perfect home for sea life, but as they travel further down, the ocean is blacker. They switch on the lights of the DeepSee and, finally, there is the bottom of the seamounts. Here they can see how the seamounts began. There's the hole of an old volcano, perhaps millions of years old. Most seamounts come from volcanoes.

After five hours, Klapfer, Stone and Skerry return to their ship and plan their next journey to the seamounts.

2.4
T = Ms Tengku, S = Mr Stewart, C = Colleague of Mr Stewart

Conversation 1
T: Mr Stewart?
S: Yes?
T: My name's Ms Tengku. Nice to meet you.
S: Nice to meet you too.
T: How was your flight?
S: Very good, thank you.

Conversation 2
T: Good morning.
S: Good morning.
T: Was your hotel comfortable?
S: Yes, it was fine, but the Internet didn't work.
T: Oh dear. Do you want to use the connection here?
S: That would be helpful, thanks.

Conversation 3
C: Hi, how's your trip?
S: It's fine so far.
C: How was your meeting?
S: Really interesting. We had a very good discussion today and we have another one tomorrow. I think we can do business with them.
C: Great!

Conversation 4
C: It's really sunny here. What's the weather like?
S: Terrible. It's rained every day. Last night there was a storm. I didn't sleep at all.

Conversation 5
S: Jane took me to an excellent restaurant last night. It was in a beautiful old building.
C: Did you try the local food?
S: Yes, it's very hot and spicy. They eat a lot of fish as well.
C: I don't think I'd like it. I don't eat hot food.
S: Yes, I drank a lot of water with it!

Unit 8

2.8

1 These women are at a festival. They are wearing colourful Indian clothes called saris and they are carrying something on their heads. But this isn't in India. It's in Oxford, England.

2 This one is obvious. It's a police officer in the United States. He has a uniform with a motorcycle helmet and white gloves. He's a Navajo police officer. That means he's from the north American Indian tribe called the Navajo Indians. They live on a place called a reservation and he works as a police officer on the reservation.

3 These two young boys are from Nepal. They are monks so they wear these special clothes. Everyone in Nepal knows they are monks because of their famous red and yellow clothes. And they have a purple robe. It's very practical and it's very warm in the cold mountains of Nepal.

4 The Masai people live in Tanzania in Africa. They are famous for their red and black clothes and this man is wearing them. He's also got long, black hair and wears jewellery around his neck.

5 This woman is from Peru. She's selling things on the side of the road in the mountains. Her clothes are traditional, with a red dress and a white hat on her head.

2.9

P = Presenter, S = Sheena Turner
P: Welcome to The Nature Show. This week's programme is about how some animals use their appearance so their enemies cannot see them. We call this camouflage and some animals are very good at it. With me to talk about this is nature expert Doctor Sheena Turner. Doctor Turner, can you give an example of an animal camouflage?
S: Yes, of course. A lot of animals are the same colour as the landscape. So, for example, a deer in the forest is difficult to see. That's because it's brown and the trees are also brown.
P: Yes. Is that true for all animals?
S: No, not at all. Zebras aren't the same colour as the landscape of central Africa but they use camouflage.
P: Zebras? But you can always see a zebra because of its black and white stripes. It's easy for a lion to see a zebra, isn't it?
S: Well, lions are colour blind, so they can't see the difference between the black and white stripes of a zebra and the brown and green landscape of central Africa. But there's a good reason for the black and white stripes. Zebras are social animals. They live in big groups. When they stand together, you can't see a single zebra.
P: Why is this important?
S: Because when a lion looks for one zebra, it can't see it. All it can see is a large group.
P: I see. Very clever. And how do other animals use their appearance?
S: Some butterflies have large, round colours on their wings. To other animals, these look like the eyes of a large animal, so they don't go near the butterfly.
P: That is good camouflage! But what animals change their appearance? For example, the chameleon can change its colour.
S: That's true, but chameleons don't change colour for camouflage. A chameleon changes colour when a dangerous animal is near because it wants to tell other chameleons about the danger. But another animal called the Arctic fox changes colour. In the winter, it is white because there is snow. In spring and summer, it's brown because there isn't snow and the landscape is brown and green.
P: That's amazing, Doctor Turner, and thank you for coming in today.

2.10

This photo shows a family, I think. On the right is the grandmother and on the left is the mother, maybe. The two children in the middle are waiting for dinner. The girl is looking at something and, in front of her, the boy is looking through a telescope. But I think it's the wrong way round! The family looks serious, but perhaps they are hungry. They are wearing special clothes. I think they are from Lapland in northern Norway because the women's hats and clothes are from this region. The photo is interesting because it shows people in their everyday life.

Unit 9

2.12

1
A = Astronaut, M = Mission control
A: I'm stepping onto the planet now. I'm down.
M: What can you see?
A: Mountains. They're very red. And there's a light about a kilometre away.
M: Is it the sun?
A: No, but it's moving closer. It's moving very fast.
M: What is it?
A: I don't know. But I'm not alone on this planet!

2
These animals live in the mountains and they usually come out at night. So we're very lucky to see the mother with her young today. They are hungry so the mother is looking for food.

3
P = Police officer, C = Criminal
P: Don't move! This is the police.
C: But I didn't take the gold.
P: I said, 'Don't move'. What are you doing at the bank?

4
M = Man, W = Woman
M: So, how are you?
W: Fine. You look great.
M: I'm older.
W: No, you look the same.
M: Well, you look older.
W: Oh.
M: But still beautiful.
W: Thanks.
M: Can I ask you something?
W: Sure.
M: Why did you leave me?

2.14
1 I'm going to the shops.
2 Chris is going to meet friends.
3 I'd like two DVDs, please.
4 They're going to make a film.
5 The film starts in two minutes.
6 She's going to watch a documentary.
7 Can I have two tickets?
8 We're going to buy tickets.

2.16
Film, music and arts news
We look at the latest news from the world of film, music and art.

Josh Roberts is going to work in Hollywood to make his next film. The young Irish film director is going to buy a house in Los Angeles to live there for two years. He said, 'I'm not going there forever.'

The band Stronger are going to be on TV next week to play their new songs. Switch on at seven on Wednesday evening to watch a TV documentary about the group.

There is going to be an exhibition of Javier Bowman's art at the National Gallery to show the artist's most famous paintings. The exhibition opens on 10th January. Phone this number 0845 4785 to book tickets.

2.17
In 1982, the author Michael Morpurgo wrote a book called *War Horse*. It was a book for children about a horse called Joey. Joey lives on a farm, but the army want horses because it is the First World War. Joey goes to France and we learn about the war through the life of Joey.

Michael Morpurgo's book was very popular and in 2007, the National Theatre of Great Britain made the book into a stage play. At the time, people didn't know how they could make a story about a horse into a play. How would they show the horse? In the theatre, the horses are giant puppets. Like the book, the play was very popular and there are theatre productions of *War Horse* in London, New York, Toronto, Australia and Germany.

War Horse became even more famous in 2011 because Steven Spielberg made a film version. Spielberg trained horses for the film. He used fourteen different horse 'actors' to play Joey. The film critics liked the film and thousands of people around the world went to the cinema to see it.

2.18
R = Richard, M = Max
R: Hi Max. It's Richard.
M: Hi Richard. Sorry, but I'm going to a meeting now so I don't have long.

R: OK, it's just that a friend gave me some free tickets for a concert. Do you want to go?
M: What is it?
R: Some music by Mozart.
M: Hmm, I don't know much about classical music.
R: I don't either but it's free, so would you like to come?
M: OK thanks, I'd love to. When is it?
R: Tomorrow night. Are you free?
M: I'm sorry, but I'm working late tomorrow night.
R: What time do you finish?
M: At seven.
R: That's OK. It starts at eight. Let's meet at seven outside your work.
M: That's great. See you at seven.

2.21
1 Would you like to go to the cinema?
2 Are you free tonight? I've got tickets for a musical.
3 Do you want to go to a concert?
4 Would you like to meet for dinner?

Unit 10

2.22
M = Manager, K = Karen
Conversation 1
M: OK, Karen. Have you ever used this machine before?
K: Yes, of course I've used one before.
M: No, I mean, have you ever made copies with this type of machine? It's different from others.
K: Oh, I see. No, I haven't, but it looks similar to the one in my previous job.

Audioscripts

Conversation 2
M: And this is yours.
K: Oh, I've never seen one like this before.
M: It's very easy. Press this button.
K: OK. I've done that.
M: Great. Has the screen come on?
K: Yes, it has.
M: Now you put your finger on the screen.

Conversation 3
K: Someone has left a message on my phone.
M: OK. Press play.
K: I have pressed play but it doesn't work.
M: Have you switched it on?
K: Ah. Sorry! No, I haven't.

2.23
1 Have you ever listened to a podcast?
2 Have you ever learned a subject online?
3 Have you ever used a sat nav?
4 Have you ever downloaded an ebook?
5 Have you ever booked a ticket online?
6 Have you ever used online banking?

2.24
a I've printed the photos.
b She hasn't sent a letter.
c They've booked tickets.
d Have you ever learned Spanish?
e No, I haven't.
f Has he sent the email?
g Yes, he has.
h It hasn't worked today.

2.25
H = Host, G = Green team, B = Blue team
H: After round four, let's look at the scores. The Green team has ten points and the Blue team also has ten points.
So, on to round five and the questions are about science and technology. Green team, it's your question first. In 1901, an Italian physicist sent a radio message across the Atlantic from England to Canada. What was his name?
G: Marconi.
H: Marconi is correct. Two points for the Green team. The next question is for the Blue team. You can send messages using a series of short and long sounds. This is a type of code. What is the name of the code and its inventor? I'll have to hurry you for an answer, Blue team.
B: Morse Code?
H: Is correct! Two points. And the next question is for the Green team. In the first century, the Chinese invented an object. It pointed north and south. What was the invention?
Do you have an answer? No? OK, Blue team, for two points. In the first century, the Chinese invented an object. It pointed north and south. What was the invention?
B: Was it the compass?
H: It was! That gives the Blue team fourteen points and the Green team twelve points.

2.26
L = Lance, S = Sophie
L: Hello, AGA Technologies. Can I help you?
S: Hello, Lance. This is Sophie.
L: Hello, Sophie. Where are you now?
S: I'm at the Science Fair in Cologne.
L: Great. What time is it there?
S: Err, it's six o'clock.
L: Is that six in the morning?
S: No, in the evening. I want to give you the name of my hotel for the next two days. It's the Insel Hotel …
L: One moment. I need a pen. OK. Was that the Ensal Hotel?
S: No, the Insel Hotel. I for Italy, N – S – E for England, L.
L: Oh sorry. Insel.
S: And the number is zero two one, eight eight three four, five zero.
L: Was that zero two one, eight eight three four, five zero?
S: That's right.

L: Is there anything else?
S: Have you emailed me a copy of the new prices?
L: No, I haven't because your email wasn't working.
S: That's strange. Can you fax it to the hotel? I don't know the number.
L: Don't worry. I've just looked at your hotel website and there's a fax number on that.
S: Great, thank you. I'll call you later. Bye for now.

2.28
1
V = Voicemail, L = Lisa
V: Hello. This is the Insel Hotel. Please leave a message after the tone.
L: Hello. This is Ms Lisa Farrell. That's F-A-R-R-E-L-L. This is a message for Doctor Nakao. That's N-A-K-A-O. I'm in Cologne tomorrow at two o'clock in the afternoon. Can I meet him in the hotel reception area. Thank you.

2
V = Voicemail, R = Richard
V: Hello. This is AGA Technologies. I'm sorry, but we are now closed. Please leave a message after the tone.
R: Hello. This is Richard Nowitz. That's N-O-W-I-T-Z. This is a message for Dan Moore in Design. Can he email me the designs before twelve o'clock tomorrow? My email is r underscore nowitz at nowitz dot com. It's very urgent.

3
V = Voicemail, M = Max
V: Hello. This is Christine. Sorry I can't answer my phone, but leave a message and I'll get back to you.
M: Hi. This is a message for Christine. My name's Max Lloyd. That's L-L-O-Y-D. You don't know me, but I'm a friend of George's. He gave me your number. I'm interested in renting the room in your apartment. Is the room still available? You can call me on 0990 768 2238 or you can email me at m thirty-six dot lloyd at hotmail dot co dot uk. Thanks. Bye.

Unit 11

2.29
1 Once I rented a motorbike, but I crashed. I was in hospital for two weeks. Fortunately, I had medical insurance so it didn't cost me anything. It's really important in case something bad happens.

2 At this time of year in Asia it's always hot, so you don't need many clothes. But it can be quite cold later in the year, so you should bring a coat for the rain and take an extra jumper.

3 I rented a car in England, but it was scary. Everybody drives on the wrong side of the road! I wanted to drive on the right and it was difficult to understand all the signs. My advice is you should take public transport! It's much easier.

4 When you go to the USA, you sometimes need a visa. Some nationalities can stay for three months without a visa, but everyone needs one to stay longer. And if you work, you definitely need to contact the US embassy in your country.

5 The first time I went to Mexico I took a phrase book. In the big cities a lot of people spoke English, but I wanted to travel to smaller towns, so I needed it there. When I got back home I took lessons in Spanish, so that next time I won't have any problems.

6 I usually change money a few weeks before I go. It's much cheaper than using an exchange office at the airport. I also carry a credit card to pay for big things like a hotel or a meal in a restaurant.

2.30
1 All passengers on flight DL3345 have to go to Gate 13 immediately.
2 You cannot carry liquids over one hundred millilitres in your bag.
3 Passengers in business class do not have to wait in this line.
4 Adults with children can get on the plane first.

2.31
1 I have to leave now.
2 We have to check in at three o'clock.
3 Do you have to go?
4 Yes, I have to.
5 Do we have to show our passports here?
6 No, you don't have to.

2.32
P = Presenter, S = Suzy Trudeau
P: The best travel experiences are when we meet local people. It's a great way to discover what a country is really like. However, if you visit someone's home, it's important to be polite, so you need to know about their customs. With me today is Suzy Trudeau. Suzy is an expert in communication skills. So, Suzy, can you give us an example of what a tourist or traveller needs to know in certain countries?
S: Sure. For example, let's imagine we are going on holiday to Greece. If you meet someone in Greece, you shake hands with both adults and children. And if you go to their house, you can take flowers or a small gift. Oh, but don't wear shoes in someone's house. Take them off at the door.
P: OK, but those things are normal in lots of countries. Is there anything very different you need to do in Greece?
S: There is one thing. Greeks love dancing. You can be in a restaurant and people start dancing. You should join in, so don't eat too much before you start dancing!
P: I see. So that's a European country. What about another part of the world?
S: OK. Let's go to South Korea. Mealtimes are also important there. Wait for the oldest person at the table to eat first. And don't cross your chopsticks.
P: What about meeting people? Do you shake hands?
S: Yes, you can, or you can also bow. This is the traditional greeting.
P: What about presents?
S: Like in Greece, flowers are a nice present. And take your shoes off in South Korea as well when you go inside someone's house.
P: What about dancing?
S: Err, actually I don't know. But South Koreans enjoy socialising. They are happy to talk about most topics, especially about sport.

2.33
E = Enzo, M = Marie
E: Marie, are you going anywhere interesting for your holiday this year?
M: I don't know, Enzo. I want to go somewhere hot and with lots of interesting places to visit.
E: Can I make a suggestion? You should go to Morocco.
M: That's a really good idea.
E: Yes, it's a beautiful place. And the public transport is good, so you could travel on your own.
M: Yes, but I'd like to meet people as well.
E: OK. Why don't you go with a tour?

M: But the disadvantage is that it's more expensive.
E: How about going on a package holiday? Often they're cheap.
M: Maybe you're right.

2.34
F = Friend, MA = Model answer
1 F: Why don't you travel on your own?
   MA: Yes, but I'd like to meet people as well.
2 F: How about going with a group?
   MA: That's a really good idea.
3 F: You should stay in a really nice hotel.
   MA: But the disadvantage is that it's more expensive.
4 F: You could go on holiday in this country. It's cheaper.
   MA: Maybe you're right.

Unit 12

2.36
1 People are moving round the Earth more than ever before. Workers from different countries go to work on other continents and experts think immigration will increase. As air travel becomes cheaper, more of us will also go on holiday overseas. However, this trend will also cause problems for tourist destinations and popular cities because there will be so many tourists.

2 For the first time, more people on Earth live in cities than in the countryside. And this trend will continue in the future. By the year 2030, there will be eight billion people on the planet and many will live in cities.

3 In the past 30 years, communication across the Earth has increased. Every year, humans have new and more powerful devices. We can watch news from other countries, text friends on the other side of the Earth and share documents with work colleagues on other continents. In the future, more and more people will use this technology and the speed of the technology will become faster and faster.

4 Will there be enough water and food in the future? That's the big question for many scientists. We need a lot of food to feed all the people and this needs a lot of water. As people need more food and farmers need more land to grow the food, we need new ways of growing food. In fact, many experts are working on this problem and they are positive about the future. They think modern farming can solve the problems of food for seven billion people.

2.37
1 I'll be 50 years old next year.
2 We'll need more water.
3 The Earth will get hotter, I think.
4 It'll rain tonight.
5 I'm sure your English will improve.
6 Will you visit me?
7 Who'll win the football match?
8 They'll move to the city.

2.38
Here is the news. Astronomers have found the nearest planet to our solar system. It orbits a star in the region of space called Alpha Centauri. That's four light years from the Earth. The planet is similar in size to Earth, but it is very close to its star. For this reason, humans could not live on it. However, stars often have more than one planet, so the discovery is exciting. It's possible that there are other planets in the same solar system.

Planets near other stars are called exoplanets and astronomers have found hundreds of them since the nineties. Using powerful telescopes, they look for a star in another solar system and then they look for planets orbiting it. Recently, astronomers found a star two thousand light years away with six planets around it, and experts think there are probably thousands or millions more exoplanets in the universe.

2.39
Good morning and thank you for coming. My name's Joel and I'm from Jamaica. Today, I'd like to talk about an important day in my country. It's called National Tree Planting Day.

First of all, National Tree Planting Day is on the first Friday of October every year. The first National Tree Planting Day was in 2002. Since then, people have planted 50,000 trees across the island.

Nowadays, everyone from schoolchildren to business people are involved in the day. They can get seeds from their local Forestry Department and they can plant the seeds in local parks and communities. Last year, I went with some students from my university and we planted new trees in the gardens of a home for old people.

In conclusion, I really think National Tree Planting Day is important. In the future, I hope other countries will have the same day. Thank you very much for listening.

IELTS practice test

🎵 2.42

Presenter: IELTS practice test. In this test, you'll hear a number of different recordings and you'll have to answer questions on what you hear. There will be time for you to read the instructions and questions, and you will have a chance to check your work. The recording will be played once only. The test is in four sections.

Now turn to Section 1 on page 100 of your book. You will hear a student called Ian telling his friend about the public library. First you have time to look at questions 1 and 2. You will see that there is also an example which has been done for you.

Now we shall begin. You should answer the questions as you listen because you will not hear the recording a second time. Listen carefully and answer questions 1 and 2.

Woman: Hi Ian. I was looking for you. Where have you been?

Ian: I went to the public library in the town centre. There's a book I need for my science project. They haven't got it at the college library, so I went to see if they had it in the public library instead. It's much bigger than the college library and I soon found what I was looking for. But they've got a really good sports section and so I decided to have a look round. I found a really good book on the history of cricket.

Woman: Gosh. I never thought of going in there. What else have they got?

Ian: Well, not just books actually. There's online access, of course, but also newspapers and magazines you can read, and a noticeboard with lots of information about local events. Actually, I saw a notice about a photography club that meets there every week – sounds interesting. There's a room there where they have lectures and meetings and stuff.

Woman: Right. I didn't know that. I'll have to go in one day.

Ian: Come with me tomorrow if you like. I'm going back to pick up a book I ordered. If they haven't got the one you want, they can get it from another library in 48 hours. So, I ordered one I need to read for my course.

Woman: Wow. That's brilliant! So, are you going to join the photography club?

Ian: I haven't decided yet. I want to ask how much it costs. So, are you going to come tomorrow?

Woman: Yeah, why not!

Presenter: Before you listen to the rest of the conversation, you have some time to read questions 3 to 10. Now listen carefully and answer questions 3 to 10.

Ian: Oh look, here's a leaflet I picked up about events at the library. You see the photography club is on Mondays, at seven thirty in the evening.

Woman: Oh, right. And look, it tells you how much you have to pay – £2.50 a week.

Ian: That's not much, is it?

Woman: No, in fact all the events are quite cheap. Look. On Tuesday evening there's a storytelling workshop at seven o'clock, and that's only £1.50.

Ian: Oh, I wouldn't be interested in that.

Woman: No, but I am. My friend Jane's really into storytelling. I must tell her. And look, on Thursday at two p.m. there's an Internet club, and that's only £1.50.

Ian: But everyone knows how to use the Internet. Who would go to that?

Woman: Well, it's in the afternoon, so it's probably for old people.

Ian: Yeah, you're right. Look, on Thursday evening there's a film club. It starts at quarter to eight. That sounds more like our sort of thing.

Woman: But look at the price – £8.50 a week. The college film club's only £5.00 and I expect they have the same films.

Ian: Yeah, you're right.

Woman: But look, on Friday, they have a poetry workshop. That's at seven forty-five too, and only £3.00. I think I'd like to go to that.

Ian: OK. And on Saturday mornings there's a course in website design. That sounds more interesting than the Internet one, and it only costs £4.75 a week.

Woman: But look, it starts at ten fifteen in the morning. You never get up before lunchtime on Saturdays! Look, there's map reading in the afternoon. That would be

	better for you. It's cheaper too – only £2.75 – and you'll be awake by then because it doesn't start till a quarter to three.	Hilary:	And another question. What should I bring with me to the interview?
Ian:	Very funny. I can get up early if I need to.	Man:	Let me see. Ah yes. I have your application form here.
Woman:	Really?	Hilary:	Do I need to bring a copy of the form?
Presenter:	Now turn to Section 2 on page 101 of your book. You will hear a woman called Hilary talking on the phone about a job interview she is going to have. First you have some time to look at questions 11 to 15. Now listen carefully and answer questions 11 to 15.	Man:	No, that's not necessary. But I see you haven't attached a photograph. So if you could bring one with you, that would be useful. Just a passport-sized one is enough.
Man:	Hello. Southdown College, personnel department. Jon speaking.	Hilary:	Oh yes, of course. Do I need to bring an identity document at all?
Hilary:	Oh, hello. My name's Hilary Brown. I've applied for a job in the accommodation office at the college.	Man:	Yes please. We have checked your qualifications online, so we don't need to see certificates or anything, but we do need to check your identity.
Man:	Ah yes, and we've invited you for interview, haven't we? On Tuesday, I think.	Hilary:	And written references?
Hilary:	That's right. Only in your voicemail message you said it would be on Monday.	Man:	We have those here on your file already. So I think that's everything. Shall I send you an invitation letter confirming all these details?
Man:	Ah, yes. Here it is. Yes, some people are coming on Tuesday and Wednesday, but your interview is actually on Monday at ten o'clock in the morning.	Hilary:	Oh, yes please. That would be great. Thank you.
Hilary:	Oh good. I was actually ringing to ask where I should come to. How do I find the personnel department? Is it in the main building?	Man:	No problem.
Man:	Well, the personnel department is in another building actually, but we're not holding the interviews here. When you arrive at the college, go to the main reception and ask for room 341. They will give you directions.	Presenter:	Before you hear the rest of the conversation, you have some time to look at questions 16 to 20. Now listen carefully and answer questions 16 to 20.
		Hilary:	And could I just ask you one or two questions about the job itself?
		Man:	Of course you can. What would you like to know?
Hilary:	I see. Thank you. And will I meet the accommodation officer? Diana Cook is her name, I think.	Hilary:	So the job title is office assistant?
		Man:	That's right.
Man:	Not on Monday, actually. One of her assistants, Howard Green, will be interviewing you, and Wendy Bright will be interviewing the people on the other days. She's the other assistant. Did you particularly want to meet Mrs Cook?	Hilary:	And what will I actually have to do each day?
		Man:	Well, the office assistant is responsible for entering data onto the computer network. There is some photocopying to do, that's the other main activity, and there will be telephone calls to deal with. But the office assistant does not deal directly with students or with the accommodation providers.
Hilary:	No, no, I just wanted to know the name of the person.		
Man:	I see.	Hilary:	I see. And the hours?

Man:	Well, it's only a part-time post. Let me see. We said ten hours a week on the advertisement.
Hilary:	Oh yes, that's right. I'd forgotten. And how much per hour would I earn?
Man:	The basic rate of pay is £8.00 per hour. If you work evenings or weekends, it goes up to £8.50, but that doesn't apply to this job, because it's just weekday mornings.
Hilary:	And do I get paid holidays?
Man:	Yes. Twenty-two days a year, plus public holidays if they fall on days when you would normally be working.
Hilary:	I see. Thank you, you've been very helpful.
Man:	That's OK.

Presenter:	Now turn to Section 3 on page 102 of your book. You will hear part of a talk about keeping rabbits as pets. First you have some time to look at questions 21 and 22. Now listen carefully and answer questions 21 and 22.
Nancy:	Hi there. I'm Nancy Ronson and the subject of my talk this evening is keeping rabbits as pets. Rabbits are very cute animals, and we often think that they make great pets, especially for young children, because they're easy to look after. But actually, they need looking after quite carefully and this takes up quite a bit of time and costs quite a bit of money. So before buying one as a pet for a child, you need to think quite carefully.

First of all, however, a few facts about rabbits. Wild rabbits are very common animals that you can find living in many parts of the world. The rabbit is very common in Europe, and is also found in Asia and Australia, but most of the world's rabbits, around 50% of them, actually live in North America. This is strange because in South America there aren't very many at all!

In the wild, rabbits live for quite a long time. The oldest wild rabbit ever recorded lived to be eighteen years old, but ten to twelve years is more normal. This surprises people. When they buy a pet rabbit, they think it's going to live for maybe five years or so, but actually pet rabbits live just as long as wild ones and so you need to think about this before you buy one. |

Presenter:	Before you hear the rest of the talk, you have some time to look at questions 23 to 30. Now listen carefully and answer questions 23 to 30.
Nancy:	So now I want to tell you exactly how much time you need to look after a pet rabbit properly and how much it costs to keep one.

First of all, don't just buy one rabbit. They feel sad and lonely living alone, that's why it's always better to buy two. So, if a child has two rabbits to look after, how long does that take? Well, I would say it's going to take one hour every day, because there are a number of things to do.

Firstly, you have to give the animals their food and water. Then it is necessary to clean the place where they live. This is something you have to do every day if you want the animals to stay well. Indeed, you need to check their basic health every single day, and make sure that they get some exercise in a safe area where they can run up and down.

So what about costs? Actually buying two rabbits in the first place is going to cost you about £50. Then having microchips fitted, to identify them if they get lost or stolen, will cost another £50. The young rabbits will then need vaccinations to protect them against common diseases – the vet has to do these – and those will cost £100.

Then your rabbit will need somewhere to live. A good rabbit house costs £250 to buy, and you do need a good one if you want your pet to be comfortable and secure. Then you need to buy equipment to go inside the house. A bowl for water costs £8 and one for food costs £12. These are the essential things, but if you want to buy other things, like toys or ramps to walk up, you could spend another £20 very easily.

The food that the rabbit eats, a mixture of green vegetables and special pellets, costs £16.36 each week. Fortunately, the water comes free, and so does the newspaper you can put down each day to help keep the house clean.

The other major expense is insurance. You need this in case your rabbit gets ill and needs to go to the vet. An insurance policy will cost £10 per month. But it is worth it because the vet can be very expensive.

Therefore, if your rabbits live for ten years, and you add up all these costs, |

	then buying two rabbits and looking after them for their whole lives will cost you an incredible £16,000! Think about that, and the time needed to look after them properly, before you go down to the pet shop to buy one!
Presenter:	Now turn to Section 4 on page 103 of your book. You will hear a sports coach giving a lecture to some students about training for a five-mile running race. First you have some time to look at questions 31 to 34. Now listen carefully and answer questions 31 to 34.
Man:	Hi there. Thanks for coming. I know that you're all planning to run the five-mile race for charity that's taking place later this term. I want to give you a training programme that will help you to develop your fitness and stamina gradually. This means running every week, or actually a combination of walking, jogging and running to begin with, so that you can build up to your target distance.
	So, what should you do each week? Well, the important thing is the time you spend training. It doesn't matter what distance you run, or how fast you run at the beginning. But what is important is to spend a fixed period of time each day.
	Now this doesn't have to be fast running. At the beginning, jogging is much better. So, what do I mean by jogging? Jogging is something you can do alone or with a partner, and if you do it with a friend you can talk as you jog. If it's difficult to talk, then you're running not jogging – so slow down! Jogging is a relaxed type of activity, it shouldn't make you feel tired or out of breath.
	Now at first, you should go jogging every day. People always ask me about other sports training, but my advice is simple. If you do, say, football training one day a week, then you still need to go jogging that day as usual, but you don't have to give up the football training!
	And people also ask me about the best place to go jogging. Well, it isn't necessary to run around a sports track. The local park is fine. And jogging on grass is much better for your feet than jogging on hard roads and pavements. It's better to be away from the traffic too!
Presenter:	Before you hear the rest of the lecture, you have some time to look at questions 35 to 40. Now listen carefully and answer questions 35 to 40.
Man:	So, how does the training programme continue? Basically the programme lasts for eight weeks. Gradually, over that time, you will do more running and less jogging, so that by weeks six and seven you're getting close to running your target distance comfortably.
	People often ask me what they should wear for this type of activity, and there are some simple rules to follow. You should wear shorts – the type that you see cyclists wearing are best – rather than the type that footballers usually wear.
	You will need good shoes, but the ones you usually wear for sports training are best. You should, however, buy special socks. There are some on the market that are specially designed for runners and they will help you to keep your feet in good condition.
	In general, don't wear clothes made out of cotton as they will make you feel too hot. There are suitable clothes for runners made in different types of man-made fibres, and they're not too expensive.
	When you're training, you need to look after yourself. For example, if you start to feel hungry this probably means that you need something to drink. Generally speaking, water is the best thing in this situation and it can be a bad idea to eat anything.
	If, however, you find that you've caught a cold, then you should stop training until you feel better. If you force yourself to continue, it will be longer before you feel better. You can soon make up for lost time once you're well again.
	OK, so before I go on to …

Answer key

Unit 1

1a (pages 4 and 5)

1
1 First name   2 Surname   3 Age   4 Job   5 Country
6 Marital status   7 Address

2
Students' own answers.

3
1 h   2 f   3 e   4 b   5 d   6 c   7 a   8 g

5
1 What's   2 name's   3 Are   4 I'm   5 I'm not   6 are
7 is   8 Are   9 isn't

6
1 are   2 Are   3 'm   4 Is   5 is   6 isn't   7 aren't   8 'm

7
1 What's your name?
2 Are you from England?
3 How old are you?
4 Are you married or single?
5 Are you a student?
6 What is your address?

8
Students' own answers.

9
1 What's   2 is not   3 I'm   4 You're   5 I'm not   6 are not

1b (pages 6 and 7)

1
a 2   b 3   c 1

2
1 c   2 b   3 b   4 c   5 c

3
1 wife   2 boys   3 son   4 daughters   5 father   6 children

4
1 Charles / Ingma   2 George / Mason   3 Ranci   4 George
5 Joanne   6 Tom   7 Julie   8 Ranci

5
1 It   2 my   3 our   4 her   5 their   6 's   7 they   8 he

6
Students' own answers.

7
1 a They're b Their   2 a He's b His   3 a Are b Our
4 a You're b Your

1c (page 8)

1
1, 3, 4, 6, 8

2
1 28   2 1.6   3 27   4 60   5 English   6 60

3
1 c   2 d   3 a   4 b   5 e

4
Students' own answers.

5
1 They live **in** the USA.
2 55% of the population work **in** agriculture.
3 We live **in** Dubai.
4 Amanda and Nigel work **in** a shop.
5 49% of the people live **in** the countryside.

1d (page 9)

2
A: H J K
B: C D E G P T V
F: L M N S X Z
I: Y
O
Q: U W
R

4
Name: Doctor T Zull   Country: Australia
Name: Beata Polit   Country: Poland

5
1 I'm from
2 Nice to meet you
3 Nice to meet you too.
4 I'd like to introduce you
5 My name's
6 where are you from?
7 Nice talking to
8 See you later.

1e (page 10)

1
1 but   2 and   3 but   4 and   5 and   6 but

2
1 a   2 b   3 d   4 e   5 f   6 c

3
Example answer:
Hi! My name's Brendan and I'm 22. I'm single and I'm a student at university. I'm from Australia but I live in Italy. I speak English and Italian. I have two brothers but no sisters.

Wordbuilding / Learning skills (page 11)

1
1 in-law   2 grand   3 step   4 first   5 sur   6 middle
7 grapher   8 graph   9 sister   10 brother   11 father

3
Students' own answers.

4
1 mother   2 billion   3 East   4 agriculture   5 million
6 niece   7 Oman   8 explorers

Answer key

Unit 2

2a (pages 12 and 13)

1
1 red, yellow   2 white, black   3 yellow, black
4 blue, yellow

2
Students' own answers.

3
1 hat   2 first-aid kit   3 torch   4 camera   5 gloves
6 map   7 mobile phone   8 compass   9 boots   10 shoes

4
1 hat   2 first-aid kit   3 map   4 shoes   5 boots

5
1 rucksack   2 maps   3 first-aid kit   4 torches
5 compass   6 gloves   7 hat   8 boots

6
1 mobile phones   2 people   3 boxes   4 torches
5 knives   6 cities   7 cameras   8 men   9 keys

7
/s/ boots, hats, maps
/z/ keys, knives, mobile phones
/ɪz/ boxes, cities, compasses

8
1 those, gloves   2 that, rucksack   3 these, keys
4 this, map

2b (pages 14 and 15)

1
1 nineteen   2 747   3 fifteen   4 five   5 1976
6 twenty-four   7 twenty-seven   8 seventy-six   9 two

2
1 T   2 F   3 F   4 T   5 T   6 F   7 F   8 T

3
1 take off   2 runway   3 hostel   4 on foot   5 cheap
6 cockpit   7 expensive   8 double

4
1 are   2 aren't   3 is   4 Is   5 isn't   6 are   7 is   8 is

5
1 on   2 next   3 the right   4 left   5 above   6 under

6
1 chair   2 rug   3 blind   4 computer   5 sofa   6 curtain
7 desk
Mystery word: cupboards

2c (page 16)

1
1 b   2 c   3 a   4 d

2
1 global   2 300   3 36   4 five million
5 furniture   6 beds, chairs, sofas   7 cupboards   8 desks
9 Sweden   10 Poland   11 restaurants   12 United Kingdom

3
1 Burberry is a British company.
2 BMW is a German company.
3 Gucci is an Italian company.
4 Sony is a Japanese company.
5 Petrobas is a Brazilian company.
6 Inditex is a Spanish company.
7 Alcatel-Lucent is a French company.
8 Google is an American company. (*or* Google is a US company.)

4
1 France, Greece, Spain
2 England, Poland, Sweden
3 Brazil, Japan, Peru
4 Canada, Germany, Italy

2d (page 17)

1
1 c   2 a   3 b

2
1 e   2 a   3 c   4 b   5 d

3
Students' own answers.

4
1 T-shirt   2 one   3 black one   4 water   5 one   6 small one
7 gloves   8 ones   9 large ones

5
1 This, that   2 These, those   3 This, that   4 These, those

2e (page 18)

1
1 slow, fast   2 expensive, cheap   3 small, large
4 useful, useless   5 modern, old

2
1 new, green   2 fast, Japanese   3 small, white
4 old, Italian   5 useful, French   6 strong, blue
7 nice, brown   8 useless, old

3
Example answers:
BUY NOW! I have a beautiful, old kitchen clock. Cheap at £5. Call 567 7456.
FOR SALE! A pair of new, red and blue roller blades. Good for children. Email j_taylor@mfs.com
SALE! Old, large English bookshelf. In good condition. Perfect for all your books! Call Jim on 657 4857.

Wordbuilding / Learning skills (page 19)

1
1 worker   2 teacher   3 saxophone   4 Brazil   5 guitarist
6 Vietnamese   7 piano   8 Spanish

2
1 ish   2 n   3 ist   4 r   5 an   6 ese   7 ian   8 er

5
1 possession   2 climber   3 furniture   4 Dutch   5 Mini

Unit 3

3a (pages 20 and 21)

1
1 d   2 f   3 h   4 g   5 a   6 e   7 c   8 b

2
1 It's five o'clock.
2 It's five minutes past seven.
3 It's quarter past nine.
4 It's twenty-five minutes past one.
5 It's half past four.
6 It's twenty-five minutes to four.
7 It's quarter to nine.
8 It's five minutes to eleven.

3
1 an airport   2 Australia   3 London   4 a train station

4
Australia   a train station
an airport   London

5
1 No   2 Yes   3 Don't know   4 No   5 Yes
6 Don't know   7 Don't know   8 Don't know

6
1 big   2 quiet   3 clean   4 beautiful   5 modern, new
6 crowded   7 intelligent / smart

7
1 small   2 dirty   3 ugly   4 uncrowded   5 old

8
1 go   2 don't have   3 don't like   4 work   5 study
6 don't eat   7 meet   8 don't live

9
1 What do you do?
2 Where do you live?
3 Do you go to work by car?
4 What time do you eat lunch?
5 Do you like shopping?

3b (pages 22 and 23)

1
a doctor   b photographer   c pilot   d sailor   e student
f teacher   g waiter   h accountant

2
1 b   2 a   3 g   4 d   5 h   6 e   7 c   8 f

3
1 studio   2 hospital   3 restaurant   4 boat
5 office building   6 university   7 airport   8 classroom

4
1 T   2 F   3 F   4 T   5 T   6 F

5
1 with   2 for   3 for   4 with

6
1 comes   2 works   3 doesn't spend   4 likes   5 studies
6 goes   7 doesn't work   8 sails

7
1 Where does Brad come from?
2 Where does he work?
3 Does he spend a lot of time there?
4 Does he like being under the water?
5 What does he study?
6 Does Gina go with him on expeditions?
7 Does she work under the water?

8
/s/ likes, starts, works
/z/ comes, goes, spends
/ɪz/ dances, finishes, teaches

3c (page 24)

1
1 B   2 A   3 C

2
1 450   2 160   3 85   4 15   5 78   6 19   7 15   8 3

3
1 seven, five, two   2 first   3 six   4 third
5 twenty   6 one hundredth

4
1 30   2 15th   3 66   4 3rd   5 80

3d (page 25)

1
1 tourist information centre   2 museum   3 park
4 car park   5 library   6 theatre   7 hotel   8 aquarium

2
1 bank   2 theatre   3 tourist information centre

3
1 B   2 C   3 A

4
1 near   2 straight   3 turn   4 Where   5 away   6 past
7 take   8 here   9 Go   10 across

3e (page 26)

1
1 Karachi   2 George   3 French   4 Monday   5 July
6 This   7 I   8 Morocco   9 Haversham   10 Grant

2
1 c   2 b   3 a   4 e   5 d

3
Students' own answers.

Wordbuilding / Learning skills (page 27)

1
1 language   2 hotel   3 park   4 office   5 time   6 centre
7 transport   8 work

2
1 first   2 friendly   3 wildlife   4 head   5 closing
6 shopping   7 public   8 office

4
1 Norway   2 Tokyo   3 Bogotá   4 Atlanta   5 China
6 Vanuatu   7 Australia   8 Moscow

Answer key

Unit 4

4a (pages 28 and 29)

1
1 play a musical instrument   2 watch films
3 meet friends   4 play computer games   5 do Tae Kwon Do
6 play tennis   7 go walking   8 go to the gym

2
1 No   2 Yes   3 Yes   4 No   5 Yes

3
1 c   2 d   3 a   4 e   5 b

4
1 swimming   2 singing   3 living   4 going   5 running
6 watching   7 fishing   8 cycling

6
1 We like listening to music.
2 Bob likes playing tennis.
3 I love learning languages.
4 They like watching football.
5 Do you like going to the gym?
6 My brother doesn't like dancing at nightclubs.
7 The twins don't like doing homework.
8 We like eating foreign food.

4b (pages 30 and 31)

1
1 D   2 B   3 C   4 A

2
1 A   2 B   3 A   4 A   5 A   6 C   7 B, C   8 A, C, D   9 C

3
1 never   2 always   3 sometimes   4 usually   5 n't often
6 often

4
1 I often read a book before I go to bed.
2 I always go to work at eight.
3 I don't often meet my family.
4 I sometimes go clothes shopping.
5 I'm always busy.
6 At work, I never take lunch breaks.

5a
a 4   b 6   c 5   d 5   e 6   f 4

5b
a John‿often travels‿abroad.
b Shannon‿and Nicole‿are‿always busy.
c He doesn't‿often have time.
d How‿often does Shannon surf?
e I read‿a newspaper‿every morning.
f Michael is‿often tired.

4c (page 32)

1
1 b   2 c   3 a   4 d   5 h   6 e   7 f   8 g

2
1 h   2 g   3 a   4 c   5 b   6 e   7 f   8 d

3
2, 3, 5, 6

4
1 F   2 T   3 F   4 F   5 T   6 F   7 T   8 T

5
1 Can you   2 can't   3 very well   4 English well   5 can
6 can't   7 well   8 How well can you

4d (page 33)

1
1 22   2 Irish and Italian   3 English, Italian and French
4 Tennis and basketball   5 Playing the guitar

2
1 d   2 g   3 f   4 b   5 c   6 h   7 e   8 a

4
1 a   2 b   3 a   4 a   5 b

5
1 speaking   2 doing   3 playing   4 painting   5 going
6 watching

6
Students' own answers.

4e (page 34)

1
1 G   2 C   3 D   4 A   5 E   6 H   7 B   8 F

2
1 at work   2 the cycling race   3 Sandy's cousin
4 Sandy   5 Alex's place of work   6 the cyclists

3
1 c   2 e   3 d   4 a   5 b   6 f

4
Example answer:
Hi Matt
I can help you. I'm good at fixing computers and printers. I can come to your office later today. Yes, I'm interested in coming to the restaurant. That sounds great. Where is it?

Wordbuilding / Learning skills (page 35)

1
1 go shopping   2 play chess   3 listen to (the) radio
4 do work   5 Read (the) article   6 meet clients
7 time (do you) spend   8 watch a DVD

2
Collocations in the text: go to work, spend all day, information shows, use computer, spend an hour a day, visit sites, play games, send emails, watch videos, do online shopping, search the Internet

3
1 Washington   2 twins   3 harp   4 polar bears
5 Germany   6 Arctic   7 highlining   8 gap year

Unit 5

5a (pages 36 and 37)

1
1 a   2 b   3 b   4 a   5 b

2
1 onions   2 peppers   3 lemons   4 raisins   5 eggs
6 milk   7 rice   8 chicken   9 lamb   10 salt

3
1 1   2 2   3 3   4 1   5 2   6 3   7 1   8 2   9 1   10 2
11 1   12 2   13 3   14 2

4
1 d   2 e   3 c   4 a   5 b

5
1 No (There isn't one good month because 'you can taste different types of cheese at every time of year'.)   2 Yes
3 Don't know   4 No   5 Yes   6 Don't know   7 Yes   8 Yes

6
1 C   2 U   3 U   4 C   5 U   6 C   7 C   8 C   9 U   10 C

7
1 some   2 an   3 a   4 any   5 any   6 a   7 an   8 some

5b (pages 38 and 39)

1
1 a lot of   2 a lot of   3 a lot of / many   4 a lot of / much
5 a lot of / many   6 a lot of / many   7 a lot of
8 a lot of / much

2
Students' own answers.

3
1 water   2 bread   3 chicken   4 juice   5 eggs
6 coffee   7 salt   8 chocolate

4
1 bag   2 bottle   3 piece   4 tin   5 cup   6 kilo   7 slices
8 bottle

5
1 d   2 b   3 e   4 c   5 f   6 a

6
1 sparkling   2 a glass   3 a kilo   4 yes, very hot   5 a bottle
6 a piece of chocolate   7 a slice   8 a tin

7
1 How much rice do you want?
2 How many apples do you want?
3 How much bread do you want?
4 How many eggs do you want?
5 How much pasta do you want?
6 How many packets of pasta do you want?
7 How much chocolate do you want?
8 How many bananas do you want?

8
1 g   2 a   3 e   4 b   5 d   6 f   7 c   8 h

5c (page 40)

1
1 a   2 c   3 b

2
1 a   2 c   3 b   4 a   5 c   6 b   7 c

3
1 b   2 a   3 d   4 e   5 c

5d (page 41)

1
1 starters   2 soups   3 main course   4 salads   5 desserts
6 drinks

2
Table 2
1 ~~glass~~ of ~~still~~ water. *bottle, sparkling*
~~Onion~~ soup *tomato*
Chicken kabsa
~~Large~~ green salad *small*
~~Cheesecake~~ *no dessert*
A cup of ~~tea~~ *coffee*

3
a Can I get you anything?
b Here is the menu.
c I'd like some water.
d I'll have a small green salad.
e Could I have the bill?
f I'd like a cup of coffee.
g That was delicious.
h Are you ready to order?
1 b   2 a   3 c   4 h   5 d   6 g   7 f   8 e

5
1 a   2 b   3 a   4 b

5e (page 42)

1
1 Mix   2 Chop   3 Pour   4 Put   5 Spread   6 Slice

2
1 shop, but you can also make
2 You need the following food: an egg, some
3 Put the flour
4 mix the egg and olive oil.
5 Next, you need a pasta machine.
6 Put the pasta
7 cut the pasta into long,

4
Example answer:
1 Put the eggs into a bowl.
2 Pour the milk into the bowl.
3 Mix the eggs and milk.
4 Pour the mixture into a frying pan and cook.
5 Put the eggs on a plate.

Wordbuilding / Learning skills (page 43)

1
1 chips   2 mobile phone   3 bill   4 lift   5 pavement
6 biscuit   7 motorway   8 petrol   9 football   10 full stop

2
1 d   2 c   3 f   4 b   5 g   6 j   7 a   8 i   9 h   10 e

3
1 petrol – gas   2 lift – elevator   3 mobile – cell
4 biscuit – cookie   5 football – soccer
6 motorway – freeway   7 bill – check   8 full stop – period

4
1 a   2 g   3 b   4 c   5 f   6 h   7 e   8 d

5
kabsa: Saudi Arabia / chicken (or fish), onion, salt, pepper, tomatoes, rice, nuts, raisins
pizza: Italy / flour, tomato, cheese, olive oil, salt
ceviche: Peru / fish, lemon juice, onions, salad
pierogi: Poland / potato, flour, mushrooms, butter, cheese

Unit 6

6a (pages 44 and 45)

1
1 earn   2 give   3 change   4 spend   5 Save

2
a 5   b 3   c 1   d 4   e 2

3
a 3   b 1   c 2

4
1 d   2 c   3 a   4 e   5 b

5
1 was   2 were   3 was   4 was   5 was   6 weren't   7 were
8 wasn't   9 was

6
1 Where were her parents from?
2 What was her father?
3 Was she interested in money?
4 How long were they on the Pacific Ocean?
5 Who was the blog popular with?

7
We stress the verb in negative sentences and questions.
2 He <u>wasn't</u> on the dollar.
3 <u>Was</u> he the President?
5 They <u>weren't</u> Spanish.
6 <u>Were</u> they artists?

8
1 in my early twenties   2 in your mid thirties
3 in her late forties   4 in our early sixties
5 in his late fifties   6 in their mid twenties

6b (pages 46 and 47)

1
1 From a TV show.   2 Yes.   3 Banking and saving money.
4 His friend.

2
1 b   2 d   3 a   4 c

3
1 a interesting b interested   2 a excited b exciting
3 a boring b bored

4
Students' own answers.

5
1 lived   2 worked   3 discovered   4 phoned   5 studied
6 paid   7 received   8 died

6
1 /t/   2 /d/   3 /ɪd/   4 /ɪd/   5 /t/   6 /ɪd/   7 /d/   8 /ɪd/
9 /d/   10 /d/   11 /t/   12 /d/

7
In 2001 I lived in France. I studied French at university. After university I wanted to live in France so I returned in 2003. I worked in a currency exchange office in Paris. I liked the job and I travelled all over the country at weekends. Last year I started a job in a bank and I married a French woman.

8
1 went   2 had   3 was   4 arrived   5 died   6 discovered
7 pulled   8 gave

6c (page 48)

1
b

2
1 c   2 a   3 a   4 c   5 b   6 a   7 c   8 a

3
1 notes   2 coins   3 cheque   4 debit card   5 credit card
6 bank transfer

6d (page 49)

1
1 a buy b sell   2 a give b take   3 a spend b save
4 a lend b borrow

2
1 No   2 Yes   3 No   4 Yes

3
1 d   2 e   3 a   4 h   5 b   6 g   7 c   8 f

4
1 ☺   2 ☹   3 ☺   4 ☹

5
Students' own answers.

6e (page 50)

1
1 Hi   2 Thanks   3 Love   4 Thank you for   5 See you
6 Best regards   7 Dear Mrs   8 Thank you very much
9 I look forward to   10 Yours sincerely

2
Example answers:
1
Hi!
Thanks for the money! Here's a cheque.
It was very useful!
See you soon
Love

2
Dear Barbara
Thank you for my time in Cologne. I was pleased with our work and I enjoyed our meal at the restaurant. See you again next year.
Best regards

3
Dear Mr Smith
Thank you very much for your interest in our holidays. Please find enclosed the brochure for our holidays.
I look forward to hearing from you in the future.
Yours sincerely

Wordbuilding / Learning skills (page 51)

1
1 basketball   2 credit card   3 Tourist information
4 mobile phone   5 armchair   6 full stop   7 roller blades
8 post office

3
1 George Washington: USA / First President of the USA
2 Frida Kahlo and Diego Rivera: Mexico / Artists
3 Arthur Honegger: Switzerland / Composer
4 Ichiyo Higuchi: Japan / Writer
5 Howard Carter: England / Archaeologist

Unit 7

7a (pages 52 and 53)

1
1 fly 2 drive 3 cycle 4 take 5 sail 6 travel

2a
Land: bicycle, car, drive, train, walk, wheels
Sea: boat, sail, ship
Air: aeroplane, fly, hot air balloon, wings

3
1 didn't survive 2 didn't stop 3 didn't return
4 didn't travel 5 didn't enter

4
1 A air   B sea   C somewhere else (space)
2 A aeroplane   B ship   C satellite

5
1 A 2 A 3 B 4 A 5 B 6 A 7 A

6
1 What did Orteig offer in 1919?
2 When did Charles Lindbergh fly from New York to Paris?
3 How long did the journey take?
4 When did five ships leave Spain?
5 Where did Magellan die?
6 At night, what did people look for in the sky?
7 How many times did it travel round Earth?
8 When did it enter Earth's atmosphere?

7b (pages 54 and 55)

1
1 d 2 b 3 a 4 c

2
1 6 million 2 3.5 3 15,000 4 200,000 5 1,000
6 13,000 7 1,500

3 and 4
1 are <u>longer</u> than any other bird
2 are <u>more dangerous</u> and difficult
3 is <u>colder</u> than other parts of the world
4 for <u>longer</u> than two hours

5
1 shorter 2 easier 3 bigger 4 busier 5 cheaper
6 sadder 7 wetter 8 nicer

6
1 cheaper 2 hotter 3 more expensive 4 faster 5 safer
6 older 7 better 8 worse

7 and 9
1 My <u>brother</u> is <u>shorter</u> than <u>me</u>.
2 <u>Walking</u> is <u>slower</u> than <u>cycling</u>.
3 I think <u>rock</u> climbing is more <u>difficult</u> than <u>surfing</u>.
4 <u>Giraffes</u> are <u>taller</u> than <u>elephants</u>.
5 <u>Camping</u> is <u>cheaper</u> than <u>staying</u> in a <u>hotel</u>.
6 <u>Canada</u> is <u>bigger</u> than <u>Iceland</u>.
7 A <u>taxi</u> is more <u>expensive</u> than a <u>public</u> <u>bus</u>.
8 <u>Cities</u> are more <u>crowd</u>ed than <u>towns</u>.

7c (page 56)

1
a 2   b 1   c 3

2
1 F 2 T 3 F 4 F 5 T 6 T 7 F 8 T

3
1 shortest 2 easiest 3 biggest 4 slowest 5 cheapest
6 fastest 7 saddest 8 nicest

4
1 highest 2 best 3 largest 4 shortest 5 most populated
6 furthest 7 easiest 8 busiest

7d (page 57)

1
1 journey 2 travel 3 trip 4 travel 5 trip 6 journey

2
1 a 2 d 3 e 4 b 5 c

3
1 a 2 b 3 b 4 c 5 a

7e (page 58)

1
1 a blog b website   2 a writer b blogger
3 a online b homepage   4 a upload b download
5 a comment b post

2
1 The bus was cancelled so we waited for the next one.
2 The flight was cancelled because the weather was terrible.
3 The food was hot and spicy so we drank a litre of water with our meal.
4 The meeting was long and boring because the managing director spoke for two hours!
5 The restaurant didn't take credit cards so I paid with cash.
6 The hotel restaurant was closed so we went into the centre of town for a meal.

3
Example answer:
I took a train across the country. We went past mountains and there was snow. Suddenly we stopped. The train couldn't move because there was snow on the line. It was night. We spent hours on the train and it was very cold. Fortunately, a man on the train had a guitar and he played songs. Everyone sang to the music. In the morning it was sunny and finally the train started moving again.

Wordbuilding / Learning skills (page 59)

1
1 The journey was very/really good.
2 The food was very/really good.
3 The meetings weren't very interesting.
4 The party was really great!
5 The weather was very/really bad.
6 It wasn't very sunny.
7 The meal was nice.
8 The hotel was really amazing!

2
1 c 2 a 3 b

4
1 They sailed to America in the *Mayflower* in the 17th century.
2 The *Mayflower II* sailed to America in 1957.
3 The *Silver Queen* took 44 days to fly from to Cape Town.
4 The saiga travels 35 kilometres per day.
5 The tree frog migrates 30 metres.
6 The loggerhead turtle travels 14,000 kilometres in fifteen years.
7 Voyager took off in 1977.
8 Jupiter is 349,000 kilometres from Earth.

Answer key

Unit 8

8a (pages 60 and 61)

1
1 boring 2 noisy 3 crowded 4 colourful 5 fun

2
1 F 2 F 3 T 4 T 5 F 6 F 7 T 8 F

3
1 eyebrow 2 eye 3 nose 4 ear 5 lips 6 cheek 7 chin

4
1 beautiful 2 short 3 curly 4 dark

5
1 have got 2 're 3 has got 4 has got 5 's

6
1 lips 2 eyebrow 3 ugly 4 mask 5 cheeks 6 straight 7 blonde 8 handsome

8b (pages 62 and 63)

1
1 b 2 e 3 a 4 c 5 d

2
1 No. 2 England. 3 The United States. 4 A reservation.
5 Red, yellow and purple. 6 It's very warm.
7 Red and black. 8 Long, black hair. 9 Selling things.
10 Her dress and her hat.

3
1 We like buying new clothes. 2 Your new dress is like mine.
3 These shoes are like my old ones. / My shoes are like these old ones. 4 I don't like my uniform.
5 This hat is like a cowboy hat. 6 Jason likes wearing jeans.

4
1 Sentences 1, 4, 6 2 Sentences 2, 3, 5

5
1 isn't wearing, 's wearing 2 's buying, isn't selling
3 isn't making, 's designing 4 isn't playing, 's reading

6
1 What's he wearing?
2 Is Trisha buying or selling clothes?
3 What is Georgio designing?
4 Is he playing a computer game?

7
1 comes 2 're staying 3 take 4 are (you) standing
5 Do (you) know 6 'm walking 7 Are (you) learning
8 Do (you) like

8
1 hat 2 dress 3 shoes/boots 4 jumper 5 shirt
6 belt 7 skirt 8 socks
Mystery word: trousers

8c (page 64)

1
1 deer ✓ 2 squirrel 3 zebra ✓ 4 elephant 5 lion ✓
6 butterfly ✓ 7 chameleon ✓ 8 polar bear 9 Arctic fox ✓
10 giraffe

2
1 Yes 2 No 3 No 4 Don't know 5 Yes 6 Yes 7 No
8 Don't know

3
1 foot 2 hand 3 neck 4 back 5 leg 6 shoulder
7 knee 8 arm

8d (page 65)

1
1 A family. 2 Dinner. 3 The boy.
4 Serious (and perhaps they are hungry).
5 Because of the women's hats and clothes.

2
1 This photo 2 On the right 3 in the middle
4 in front of her 5 The family looks 6 They are wearing
7 I think 8 The photo is interesting

4
1 t 2 w 3 d 4 b 5 h 6 k 7 e 8 n

8e (page 66)

1
1 UR 2 4u 3 CU 4 2day 5 b4 6 Weds 7 @ 8 RU
9 GR8 10 pls 11 l8 12 sry 13 thx 14 <3 15 4get
16 atm 17 :-) 18 w/e

2
1 pls come on weds
2 RU :-) 2day?
3 Sry I'm l8
4 R we meeting @ w/e?
5 I <3 the film
6 I have GR8 news!
7 Call me b4 U leave
8 CU l8er

3
Example answer:
A: Sry I'm l8 :-(
B: Where RU?
A: On the train atm. Where RU?
B: I w8ing 4U @ the cinema
A: Can we meet l8er?
B: What time?z
A: @ 2?
B: 2 is ok. I'll w8 in the café
A: OK. CU there.
B: tks

Wordbuilding / Learning skills (page 67)

1
1 Put on 2 get up 3 eat out 4 Look at 5 turn off
6 Go back 7 Take off 8 look up

3
T: put on, look at, turn off, take off, look up
I: get up, eat out, go back

4
1 In the Philippines. 2 'Capgrossos' or large masks.
3 In Papua New Guinea. 4 In ice. 5 Tattoos.
6 Chris Rainier. 7 Reinier Gerritsen. 8 Emoticons.

Unit 9

9a (pages 68 and 69)

1
1 actor   2 actress   3 screen   4 audience   5 front row
6 aisle   7 back row   8 seat

2
1 romantic comedy   2 horror   3 documentary
4 animation   5 Science fiction   6 comedy

3
1 d   2 b   3 c   4 a

4
1 a   2 b   3 a   4 c   5 a   6 b   7 c   8 c

5
1 d   2 b   3 e   4 c   5 f   6 a

6
1 'm going to watch   2 're going to play   3 's going to buy
4 's going to meet   5 're going to have   6 're going to make

7b
1 /tə/   2 /tə/   3 /tu:/   4 /tə/   5 /tu:/   6 /tə/   7 /tu:/   8 /tə/

9b (pages 70 and 71)

1
1–3 actor, audience, musical
4–7 actor, audience, film, screen,
8–9 artist, painting
10–12 audience, music, musicians
13–14 novel, writer

2
●●: artist, novel, painting, theatre, writer
●●●: actresses, cinema, gallery, musical
●●●: director, musician

3
1 e   2 c   3 d   4 h   5 a   6 g   7 b   8 f

4
1 I'm going to borrow this book to read about film-making.
2 I'm going to download this song to listen to it.
3 I'm going to book tickets to see a play.
4 I'm going to buy this film to watch it later.
5 I'm going to evening classes to learn French.
6 I'm going to drama school to study acting.

5
1 to make his next film
2 to live there for two years
3 to play their new songs
4 to watch a TV documentary
5 to show the artist's most famous paintings
6 to book tickets

9c (page 72)

1
1 butterflies   2 trees   3 fruit   4 kangaroos   5 mountains
6 leaves   7 Rock   8 sea

2
The book: 1   The play: 2   The film: 3

3
1 T   2 F   3 T   4 T   5 F   6 T   7 F   8 T

9d (page 73)

1
1 To a meeting.   2 They are free.   3 Tomorrow night.
4 He's working late.   5 At seven.   6 Outside Max's work.

2
1 Do you want   2 would you like to   3 I'd love   4 Are you
5 I'm sorry   6 Let's meet   7 That's   8 See you

3
1 ☺   2 ☹   3 ☺   4 ☹

4
Students' own answers.

5
1 're meeting   2 'm wearing   3 're going   4 are you going
5 's talking   6 'm not taking   7 's working
8 aren't playing

6
1 F   2 P   3 F   4 P   5 P   6 F   7 F   8 P

9e (page 74)

1
1 loud   2 worried   3 well   4 very old   5 beautiful
6 delicious

2
1 sounds   2 tastes   3 feels / felt   4 look   5 smells

3
Example answers:
1 The Alhambra is a new Middle Eastern café in the centre of town. Its sandwiches taste delicious. There's a nice mix of old and new furniture and the staff are very friendly.

2 *War Horse* is a play at the theatre about a horse called Joey in the war. The horse looks amazing on stage and also it's a really interesting story. My only negative comment is the music. It sounds very loud.

3 *Digital Hero II* is a new computer game. The graphics on the screen look modern but I felt a bit bored at times. I think that's because it isn't very different to *Digital Hero I*.

Wordbuilding / Learning skills (page 75)

1
1 student   2 musician   3 writer   4 painter   5 explorer
6 artist   7 director   8 manager

2
1 watching   2 listen   3 on   4 at   5 much   6 play
7 interesting   8 handsome

3
a 4   b 6   c 7   d 1   e 8   f 2   g 3   h 5

Unit 10

10a (pages 76 and 77)

1
1 technology 2 astronomy 3 zoology 4 biology
5 physics 6 chemistry 7 neuroscience

2
1 physics 2 astronomy 3 technology 4 zoology
5 neuroscience

3
1 a download b CD 2 a library b search engine
3 a map b sat nav 4 a podcast b radio 5 a text b send

4
1 c 2 a 3 b

5
1 Have you ever used 2 've used 3 have you ever made
4 haven't 5 've never seen 6 've done 7 has 8 has left
9 have pressed 10 Have you switched 11 haven't

6
Students' own answers.

7
a 4 b 5 c 3 d 5 e 3 f 5 g 3 h 4

8
a I've printed the photos.
b She hasn't sent a letter.
c They've booked tickets.
d Have you ever learned Spanish?
e No, I haven't.
f Has he sent the email?
g Yes, he has.
h It hasn't worked today.

10b (pages 78 and 79)

1
1 b 2 d 3 a 4 c

2
1 Reason 1: as a historic city with lots of interesting places to visit. Reason 2: for difficult roads.
2 Because visitors become lost in the old streets.
3 In 1865. 4 Two years. 5 No. 6 No.
7 The hippocampus. It's the part that stores memories.
8 It's bigger than in the brains of other people.

3
1 a 2 c 3 a 4 c 5 b

4
1 buy 2 bought 3 paid 4 put 5 sent 7 forget
8 made 9 read 10 win

5
1 read 2 won 3 buy/win 4 send 5 put/read
6 paid 7 forgotten

6
1 Have, taken, took 2 Have, studied, studied
3 Have, taught, taught 4 Have, learned, learned
5 Have, written, wrote

10c (page 80)

1
1 iPod 2 vacuum cleaner 3 wheel 4 knife 5 electricity
6 sticky tape 7 fire 8 Internet

2
a 3 b 1 c 6 d 7 e 2 f 5 g 4 h 8

3
First question: c
Second question: a
Third question: b

4
1 Ten points. 2 In 1901. 3 They are short and long.
4 In the first century. 5 North and south. 6 Blue team.
7 Fourteen. 8 Twelve.

10d (page 81)

1
1 a 2 c 3 a 4 b 5 b

2
1 g 2 b 3 d 4 e 5 a 6 h 7 c 8 f

3
1 three 2 Insel 3 A 4 afternoon 5 seven

10e (page 82)

1
1 at 2 dot com 3 slash 4 dash 5 www dot
6 double slash 7 colon 8 dot org 9 underscore
10 dot co dot uk

2
1 h_schmitt@hotmail.co.de
2 www.concordia.com
3 www.instolisten.org/dailypod-2

3
1 Call Stacey back.
2 Send everyone a letter.
3 Take Mr D'Souza to the station.
4 Book a table for two.
5 Buy more paper.
6 Print these photographs, please.
7 Email the designs to g_rich@gmail.com.
8 Telephone the hotel.

4
1 Name of caller: Lisa Farrell
  Message for: Dr Nakao
  Message: Meet her in the hotel reception at 2pm.
2 Name of caller: Richard Nowitz
  Message for: Dan Moore
  Message: Email the designs before 12 tomorrow.
  His email is r_nowitz@nowitz.com
  Urgent ✓
3 Name of caller: Max Lloyd
  Message for: Christine
  Message: Friend of George. He's interested in renting the room. Call him on 0990 768 2238 or email him: m36.lloyd@hotmail.co.uk

Wordbuilding / Learning skills (page 83)

1
1 send 2 Study 3 memorise 4 Search 5 show 6 find
7 call 8 stop working

2
1 a forget b remember 2 a take b leave 3 a teach b learn
4 a receive b send

4
Example answers:
a biology, technology, zoology
b email, text, letter
c email, search engine, satellite navigation
d public telephone, postcard, sticky tape

Unit 11

11a (pages 84 and 85)

1
1 camping   2 sightseeing   3 backpacking   4 hiking

2
1 return ticket   2 sightseeing   3 check in, carry on   4 rent
5 tour guide   6 souvenirs   7 book

3
1 Yes   2 Yes   3 Don't know   4 No   5 Don't know   6 Yes
7 Yes   8 No

4
1 b   2 e   3 f   4 c   5 d   6 a

5
1 should   2 shouldn't   3 should   4 should   5 shouldn't
6 should

6
1 You should book a hotel room.
2 He shouldn't work late.
3 Should we buy a ticket here?
4 She should check in her bag.
5 You shouldn't rent a car.
6 What should we eat?

7
Hi!
I've booked my tickets and I'm arriving on the 21st! Before I arrive at your house, I'm going to travel round the country. Should I rent a car or go by public transport, do you think? Also I'm going to spend some time in the capital. What should I see there? And should I book my hotel in advance? Can you give me any advice? Oh! And what's the weather like? Is it cold? Should I bring lots of clothes?
See you soon!
Mike ☺

8
Example answer:
Dear Mike
I'm really happy that you are coming to my country. Here is my advice:
When you travel round the country, you should go by public transport because it's cheaper than a car and there are lots of buses and trains.
In my capital city, you should see the parliament buildings and the old castle.
For hotels, I think you should book the hotel online. It's very easy.
At the moment the weather is very cold, so you should bring a warm coat!
See you soon!

11b (pages 86 and 87)

1
1 e   2 b   3 a   4 f   5 d   6 c

2
1 A motorbike.   2 No.   3 Asia.   4 A coat and a jumper.
5 England.   6 People drive on the left (or 'the wrong side') and the signs were difficult to understand.   7 Everyone.
8 The US embassy in your country.   9 A phrase book.
10 In smaller towns.   11 Before.   12 For 'big things' like a hotel or a meal in a restaurant.

3
Across: 1 climate   3 visa   5 zones   6 licence   7 cultural
Down: 1 currency   2 hand   4 illegal

4
1 a   2 c   3 b   4 c   5 c   6 a   7 b   8 a

5
1 flight DL3345 have to go to
2 You cannot carry, in your bag.
3 in business class do not have to wait in
4 with children can get on the plane

6
1 /hæftə/   2 /hæftə/   3 /hæftə/   4 /haef tuː/   5 /hæftə/
6 /haef tuː/

11c (page 88)

1
They talk about Greece and South Korea.

2
1 Do   2 Do   3 Don't   4 Do   5 Don't   6 Don't   7 Do
8 Do

3
1 thing   2 where   3 body   4 thing   5 body   6 where
7 thing   8 body

4
1 anybody   2 something   3 nowhere   4 Everything
5 everybody   6 somewhere   7 Somebody   8 anything

11d (page 89)

1
1 F   2 T   3 T   4 F   5 T   6 T   7 F (Marie thinks it's expensive.)   8 F

2
1 Can I make a suggestion?
2 You should go to Morocco.
3 You could travel on your own.
4 Why don't you go with a tour?
5 How about going on a package holiday?

3
a 5   b 4   c 2   d 3

5
1 bus /ʌ/   2 book /ʊ/   3 you /uː/   4 but /ʌ/   5 should /ʊ/
6 food /uː/   7 cruise /uː/   8 could /ʊ/

11e (page 90)

1a
1 Did   2 Was   3 How many   4 How   5 Would   6 Were
7 What   8 Why

1b
a 3   b 1   c 4   d 2   e 5   f 8   g 6   h 7

Wordbuilding / Learning skills (page 91)

1
1 manager   2 photograph/photo   3 photographer
4 study   5 backpacker   6 visit   7 visitor   8 cook
9 design   10 designer

2
1 manage   2 photograph/photo   3 student   4 backpack
5 visitor   6 cooker   7 designer

3
photograph (3) / photo (2) photographer (4)
backpack (2) backpacker (3)
visit (2) visitor (3)
study (2) student (2)
cook (1) cooker (2)
design (2) designer (3)

4
1 b   2 a   3 f   4 c   5 d   6 e

Answer key

Unit 12

12a (pages 92 and 93)

1
1 Arctic Circle 2 North Pole 3 Northern hemisphere
4 Equator 5 Antarctic Circle 6 South Pole 7 Southern hemisphere

2
1 c 2 b 3 e 4 a 5 f 6 d

3
1 14,000,000km^2 2 0°C 3 2.5 l 4 30% 5 130m
6 419,455kg

4
1 e 2 a 3 d 4 b

5
1 a 2 b 3 c 4 b 5 c 6 a 7 c 8 a

6
1 cars will   2 houses will   3 children won't
4 the summer won't   5 the winter will   6 people won't

7
1 'll 2 'll 3 will 4 'll 5 will 6 will 7 'll 8 'll

12b (pages 94 and 95)

1
1 island   2 Ocean   3 forest   4 mountain   5 Lake   6 Sea
7 River   8 Desert

2
1 the 2 the 3 Ø 4 Ø 5 Ø 6 the 7 Ø 8 Ø 9 the
10 Ø 11 the 12 Ø 13 the 14 the 15 the

3
2 Which ocean is ~~the~~ Madagascar in?
4 Where is ~~the~~ Lake Vostok?
6 Where is ~~the~~ Mount Ararat?

5
1 b 2 d 3 a 4 c 5 e

6
1 old 2 high 3 tall 4 well 5 long 6 fast 7 far

7
1 43   2 39km   3 100m   4 really well   5 ten minutes
6 1,342km/h   7 31km

12c (page 96)

1
1 star 2 planets 3 orbit 4 Astronomers 5 surface
6 rock 7 travel

2
1 c 2 a 3 d 4 b

3
1 Astronomers 2 orbits 3 Earth 4 humans
5 discovery 6 exoplanets 7 star 8 planets   9 universe

12d (page 97)

1
1 Jamaica.   2 The first Friday.   3 50,000   4 Everyone from schoolchildren to business people.   5 In local parks and communities.   6 In the gardens of a home for old people.   7 Have the same day.

2
1 c 2 g 3 b 4 a 5 f 6 d 7 e

3
1 Today, I'd like to talk about an important day.
2 First of all, my country's national day is on 4th July.
3 Since then, people have always celebrated this day.
4 Nowadays, everyone has a day off.
5 Next, families have a big meal together.
6 In conclusion, I really think it's important.

12e (page 98)

1a
Possible answers:
1 Everyone ~~is~~ invited ~~to our~~ New Year's Party!
2 ~~The~~ Annual Party ~~is~~ at ~~the~~ Town Hall on 1st May.
3 ~~There is a~~ huge sale at ~~the~~ Big Bed Shop ~~all~~ this week.
4 ~~You can~~ eat delicious sandwiches at Jill's Café.
5 Visit ~~the website~~ www.greenfest.org for details.
6 ~~The~~ entrance to ~~the~~ disco ~~is~~ free.
7 ~~Listen to~~ live music and ~~look at~~ local art at ~~the~~ Mayberry Arts Festival.
8 ~~You are~~ welcome to ~~our~~ Midsummer Party at nine.

b
Possible answer:
You are invited to <u>plant a tree on 7th October</u> for <u>National Tree Planting Day</u>. We will give you <u>free seeds to plant in the local park</u>. There will be <u>lots of people</u> there and <u>lots of entertainment</u>, so <u>bring the whole family</u>. We'll have <u>hot and cold food</u>, and <u>local shops</u> will sell <u>environmentally friendly products</u>. We'll also have <u>presentations</u> about <u>how to help the environment</u> and <u>information about gardening</u>. The event is in <u>Tenant Park</u>, and it starts at <u>two o'clock</u> and it <u>finishes</u> at <u>five o'clock</u>. The <u>entrance is five euros for adults</u> and <u>free for children under 16</u>. You can <u>telephone</u> us on <u>088 678 4955 for more information</u>.

Wordbuilding / Learning skills (page 99)

1
1 depth 2 height 3 weight 4 length 5 width

2
1 a long b length   2 a height b high   3 a weight b weigh
4 a deep b depth   5 a wide b width

3
Adjectives: long, high, deep, wide
Verb: weigh* (note the adjective for weigh/weight is 'heavy')

6
1 914 trillion litres – the Earth's rainfall every day
2 47 metres – the depth of the Black Hole of Andros
3 2009 – the year James Cameron made the film *Avatar*
4 18 trillion – distance in kilometres between the Earth and Gliese 581g
5 20 million – the number of people at the first Earth Day in 1970

IELTS practice test

Listening
1 C I saw a notice about a photography club
2 B I'm going back to pick up a book I ordered.
3 Tuesday On Tuesday evening there's a storytelling workshop
4 £1.50 and that's only £1.50
5 Internet on Thursday at two p.m there's an Internet club
6 Thursday on Thursday evening there's a film club
7 £8.50 look at the price – £8.50 a week
8 7.45 That's at seven forty-five too
9 Website on Saturday mornings there's a course in website design
10 £2.75 It's cheaper too – only £2.75
11 A your interview is actually on Monday
12 A When you arrive at the college, go to the main reception …
13 B Howard Green … will be interviewing you
14 B/F we do need to check your identity.
15 F/B a photograph … if you could bring one with you, that would be useful
16 photocopying There is some photocopying to do
17 (tele)phone calls and there will be telephone calls to deal with
18 10 / ten ten hours a week
19 £8.00 The basic rate of pay is £8.00 per hour.
20 22 days Twenty-two days a year
21 C most of the world's rabbits … live in North America
22 B but ten to twelve years is more normal
23 one hour it's going to take one hour every day
24 clean It is necessary to clean the place where they live
25 health you need to check their basic health every single day
26 £50 Having microchips fitted will cost another £50
27 £250 A good rabbit house costs £250 to buy
28 Equipment Then you need to buy equipment to go inside the house.
29 £12 one for food costs £12
30 month £10 per month
31 C what is important is to spend a fixed period of time each day
32 B a relaxed type of activity
33 A you don't have to give up the football training
34 B The local park is fine and jogging on grass is much better for your feet.
35 eight weeks the programme lasts for eight weeks
36 cyclists the type that you see cyclists wearing
37 socks You should buy … special socks.
38 cotton don't wear clothes made out of cotton as they will make you feel too hot
39 drink this probably means that you need something to drink …
40 cold If … you've caught a cold, then you should stop training until you feel better.

Reading
1 C six days a week
2 C £5.50 per hour
3 E weekly bus ticket to the city centre provided
4 B free meals when on duty
5 B uniform provided
6 A supermarket cashier
7 C ability to speak French or Spanish an advantage
8 F temporary contract (six weeks)
9 D possibility of extra hours next month
10 C you have to work in a team
11 TRUE carried out a survey … as part of their course
12 TRUE city residents … a sample of local inhabitants
13 FALSE asked them all the same questions
14 NOT GIVEN
15 FALSE About 12% of the people they asked
16 TRUE In second place in the list was swimming … and in third place came keep-fit exercises
17 FALSE a few very keen walkers who go for long walks in the countryside
18 TRUE walking holidays are the most popular of all
19 FALSE There were an equal number of men and women going on walking holidays
20 FALSE Boating holidays … are the ones where you find the largest number of single people.
21 viii Cycling holidays are much greener than holidays by car, train or plane
22 ix a company which makes all the arrangements in advance
23 v It's up to you what distance you want to cover every day
24 i It isn't necessary to be very strong to ride a bike, but you should be in good health.
25 ii a range of options when it comes to how long to stay away and how to make sure you have a bed for the night
26 iv Holiday companies sometimes arrange for your suitcases to be sent on … This means that you only need to carry a few things
27 iii How much your holiday costs will depend on which type you choose.
28 Scotland Cycling in Scotland, for instance, where there are lots of hills, will give you a good physical workout. But if that sounds too much like hard work
29 centre-based where you return to the same hotel every evening and can have a good meal and a shower
30 March March is the typical month for the birds to arrive.
31 July back again … normally in July
32 C The young cuckoos are born in England.
33 C all spent the winter in the Congo region of central Africa
34 A Lyster flew across France, Spain and Morocco before crossing the Sahara desert
35 B Lyster flew back to England via Algeria … Chris also crossed the Algerian desert
36 C They put a tiny satellite tag on each bird's back to see where they went when they left England.
37 B The three other birds did not return to England and the scientists think they died on their return journey.
38 C the five tagged birds all travelled about 10,000 miles that summer.
39 C Algeria were countries that the other three birds flew over … Chris/Lyster flew back … via Algeria
40 A Lyster flew across Spain … flew back via Algeria … but this time didn't fly over Spain